Compost Flower Growing

SUTTON'S GIANT DOUBLE ZINNIAS

Compost
Flower Growing

S. A. BROWN

THE GARDEN BOOK CLUB
121 CHARING CROSS ROAD
LONDON, W.C.2

First published by W. Foulsham & Co. Ltd. 1960

The Frontispiece of this book is reproduced by kind permission of Messrs. Sutton & Sons Ltd., The Royal Seed Establishment, Reading, England and the monochrome photographs by permission of Messrs. Dobbie & Co. Ltd., Edinburgh.

PRINTED IN GREAT BRITAIN

By Charles Birchall & Sons Ltd., Liverpool and London.

Compost Flower Growing

Contents

CHAPTER I

The Soil and the Flower Garden. Compost making in the small garden. Some materials used for Compost making. Using Farm Yard Manure, Poultry Manure and Sewage Sludge in Compost Making. Activators, Lime and Wood Ashes. Using Compost in the Flower Garden. Animal Manures, and other organic materials used by themselves. Green Manures. No Digging Methods. Proprietary organic manures.

CHAPTER II

Planning and Lay out. Some Soil Cultivations. Initial work and planning with Herbaceous Borders, Lawns, Flower Borders and Beds. The New Rock garden. Planning for Seasonal Display. Keeping down costs. Some Plants for a Shaded Border.

CHAPTER III

Flower Garden Management. Summary of the main operations involving Annual Borders, Spring and Summer flowering Bedding Plants, Herbaceous Borders, Lawns and Rock Gardens, throughout the year.

CHAPTER IV

Special Crops. Border Carnations. Dahlias. Early Flowering Chrysanthemums, Roses. Sweet Peas.

CHAPTER V

Bulbs and Corms, grown out of doors, and in pots or bowls.

CHAPTER VI

Plants in and Around the Home. Pot Plants in the Home, dealing with their management, points on Christmas Pot Plants, Some Pot Plant Problems. Some Fuchsia Pointers, Miniature Roses as Pot Plants. Impatiens, Watering, Feeding, Care of House Plants. Hanging Baskets, and Window Boxes.

CHAPTER VII

The Small Greenhouse and Conservatory. General Points in Management for Flowers, Growing Pot Plants, Raising Bedding Plants, Growing Chrysanthemums. Taking Cuttings. Use of a Conservatory for Pot Plants. Some Popular Pot Plants. Use of a Frame for Flower Growing.

CHAPTER VIII

Plants to Grow. A Selection of 22 Herbaceous Plants. A Selection of 20 Hardy Annuals. Spring Flowering Bedding Plants. Summer Flowering Bedding Plants. A selection of 20 good subjects for the Rock Garden.

CHAPTER IX

Pests and Diseases of Flower Crops. Principles of Pest Control. Biological Methods. Handpicking. Some Pests of Flower Crops, Sucking Insects, Caterpillars, Soil Pests. Other Pests. Fungus Diseases, Soil Diseases and Virus Troubles.

CHAPTER X

Weed Control in the Flower Garden. General Points. Mulches as a Weed Control. Weeds on Lawns. Weeds on Paths. Special Weed Problems.

Chapter I

The Soil and the Flower Garden.

For all practical purposes, soil is either heavy or light, or somewhere in between. The two extremes, however, present their own problems and, with flower gardening in mind particularly, the following practical points concerning the management of each will be helpful.

A very heavy clay soil is difficult to work, cold in "nature", less well drained and gives slower growth in spring than do most other soils. It may go very hard in dry weather and can crack badly, thus leading to loss of soil moisture. The very "close" nature of the clay particles makes such a soil sticky when wet, less well aerated, harder to dig, and manage generally.

The application of compost to such a soil is a necessity. It has the effect of keeping the clay particles apart, making for better aeration and drainage, and easier working, as well as providing food material. One application of compost, of course, will not bring about this transformation. Several regular dressings are needed to bring about a complete change but even the first application starts to remedy the position. If such a soil is being dug for the first time, the addition of straw, or strawy manure, or other coarse organic material helps considerably. Surface applications of compost are described in many places later in this book, as well as the full use of mulches.

With a very light sandy soil, the disadvantages are, such free drainage that there is little moisture retention when it is most needed in summer, and the leaching out of food materials and humus by winter rains. What compost does here is to give "body" to such soil; it also makes it more water retentive, gives humus and retained food material, and takes away the "hungry" character. Maximum use should be made of green manure crops, as well as normal applications, under these conditions.

The value of earthworms in a soil is well known, and the sure method of increasing their numbers is by using compost. On a heavy soil particularly, the beneficial effect of worms is doubly valuable, as the aeration is much increased, and the natural drainage also, as well as the soil being improved by

10

organic material being passed through the bodies of the worms. The fact that worms are present in a soil is a good sign; if there are none or very few, the need for generous compost applications is acute.

Compost Making in the Small Garden.

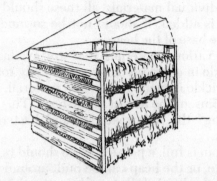

Fig. 1.—Compost bin for the small garden

A wooden bin (see Fig. 1), made from rough uncreosoted timber, with a sloping lid to keep off rain, facilitates compost making. The size of the bin should be 4ft. or 5ft. long, 4ft. wide, and 4ft. high, and one side should be movable. It should be bottomless. The pieces of timber used in the sides should not be touching, gaps should be left between them for ventilation. At least two bins will be needed, for the small garden, when compost making is well under way.

Start the heap by placing a 6in. layer of rough material at the base. Thick flower stalks can be used for this purpose, as can hedge clippings, or even twiggy, woody material, the aim being to admit air to the heap, this being a very important factor.

Usually for small scale composting one has to add one layer of compost material at a time, as it becomes available. As stressed elsewhere, I like to have, for example, a layer of lawn mowings, then a layer of straw, or green vegetable matter. Every 6ins. or so, sprinkle on a little lime, and use an activator at the maker's directions (as described under "Activators" later in this chapter).

11

If a variety of materials come to hand altogether, then all can be mixed into the heap at one time. If, as I find is the case, one only gets small amounts of material, sometimes at intervals, the layer method has to be adopted. To prevent "caking" of any one ingredient, mix the layers with a fork every 7 to 10 days or so, or every 12 to 15ins. of the height of the heap.

The amount of water to add depends on the moisture content of the individual materials, all these should be just moist. When water is added, it should not be so much that it runs away from the base of the heap.

When the various materials that are available are being added, sprinkle in a forkful or two of already rotted compost, and let this trickle in amongst the new material, as it is added, every 12 to 15ins. of the height of the heap. This has the effect of "inoculating" the new material, and hastens the rotting down process.

When the bin is full, a pointed stake should be driven down into the centre, or the heap can be built around a stake left in position until the bin is full. In either case this gives ventilation. Finally coat the top surface with 2ins. of soil, before the lid of the bin is placed in position, and plug the ventilation hole with straw.

After a few days, the heap will begin to heat up, perhaps to 150 degrees F. or more. High temperature fermentation will go on for about three weeks, during which time weed seeds and disease spores should be killed. After about a month, the temperature falls, and the heap can be turned, and water added to any dry areas. Some heating may occur after re-stacking, but the temperature soon falls. For this turning utilise the second bin—no central ventilation hole is needed at this stage. At the end of the second month, the compost is cold, and can now be left for a further month to mature, at the end of which time the contents of the heap should be dark and rich, and a valuable material for the flower garden.

The rate at which a heap made up of several ingredients will decompose depends on the time of year. In the summer good results can be obtained in three months, but the composting process is slower at other seasons.

In autumn and early winter, when one is "clearing up", the greatest bulk of compost material may be available. Old flower stems and foliage add a considerable amount of green matter to the compost heap but, here again, use it before it becomes woody. If the stems are long, cut them into pieces about 3 inches long, and make sure they are well wetted. Try not to place too thick a layer at one time; 4ins. is plenty in my experience.

Difficulty is sometimes experienced with composting the stems of herbaceous plants. I find it best to chop them up into small pieces, and to place them in a thin layer on the heap, watering and putting other materials in alternate layers. The stems are best composted whilst semi-green, that is, not allowed to become too dry before being used, but much depends on when the border can actually be attended to, as the "clearing up" may be delayed until well into winter.

Some Materials used for Making Compost.

General Points.—In a small garden, and especially where flowers only are grown, the range of material for compost making may not be very extensive. Apart from making fullest possible use of such material that is available, any of the following should be considered and advantage taken of their availability, as applicable.

Bracken.—In country areas, one may have access to this very leafy material which, cut green, in June and July, chopped up and mixed in with other vegetable material, makes a valuable addition to the compost heap. If used later in the season, the stalks may be rather woody, but if they are set aside, then chopped up and well watered, they too can be rotted down further and made good use of in the heap.

Domestic Wastes.—Any old scraps of wool or cotton material, after being well wetted, can be rotted down quite well, but keep such material in the centre of the heap. Carpet sweepings and material from the vacuum cleaner can also be used to advantage. If large items, like old trousers are used, cut these into small pieces first, wet them well before composting and use a little at a time for best results.

Hedge Trimmings.—Soft, young clippings make an excellent compost heap ingredient, but here again, use the clippings as fresh as possible; avoid having them dried up and withered before use. Late in the season, if rather more woody material is available, compost as much as is practicable and burn the remainder, thus providing one source of potash.

Kitchen Waste.—Vegetable trimmings, cabbage leaves, surplus lettuce, orange peel, tea leaves, in fact any waste vegetable matter should be utilised in compost making. I find the best way is to keep a lidded container separate for this material, and to spread a layer on my compost heap as available, but to cover this with whatever material is on hand at the time, or with 1 inch of soil, to prevent attracting birds.

Old Newspapers.—I have used these with good results in the bottom of sweet pea trenches, but all paper used in this way should be well wetted as an aid to rotting. Small quantities of newspaper will rot down in a compost heap quite well—best of all, I find, if some poultry manure can be mixed in with it.

Lawn Mowings.—I shall stress the value of this material, as a mulch, in Chapter 3, but for composting it is excellent, as it heats up well and helps in rotting down other vegetable matter in the heap. I like to have a 3in. layer, then something else, then more lawn mowings, and so on. Lawn mowings and straw go very well together, but make sure that the latter is well wetted before being composted.

It is best to use lawn mowings as fresh as possible, for if they are just tipped in a heap by themselves and left, they "go to nothing" very quickly. If sufficient quantity of straw, leaves or other material is available, a very good compost can be made with such organic matter, and lawn mowings, in equal parts, plus an activator. In a small garden, especially where flowers are the chief crops grown, the compost heap may well have to be made up of whatever materials are to hand, probably in small quantities. It is here, I feel, that lawn mowings are especially valuable. In very dry spells, the mowings are best left on the lawn itself, but apart from this every opportunity should be taken to save all the mowings available. I have seen rye grass sown on a rough patch of empty ground

14

in a new garden, just for the "mowings", such material being extremely valuable in a new garden where compostable material may be in short supply.

Leaf Mould.—If there are trees nearby, or if one has access to woodland, leaf mould is a valuable material for increasing the supply of organic material in the soil. If there are sufficient leaves to make up into a heap separately, these should be bounded by wire netting "walls" to keep them in place. It is best to weigh them down with planks, or some soil, and to wet them well as they are gathered into the heap, otherwise they are slow to rot down. If a heap is made of leaves alone, let it stand for two years, if possible, before use.

Mature rotted leaf mould can be used in potting composts, and should be rubbed through a ½in. mesh sieve for this purpose, but for forming part of a seed sowing compost, use a ⅛in. sieve. The rougher material can be placed in the bottom on the seed trays, in a layer ¼in. thick.

In small quantities leaves can also form a very useful part of the compost heap proper, in autumn, and each layer should be alternated with heavier material, such as soil, to keep them in place.

Sawdust.—Although slow to decay, sawdust has a place in the list of compost ingredients if used in small quantities at a time. My own method is to leave the sawdust to weather, for a year, and then to sprinkle thin layers into the heap, not more than a ½in. thick layer at any one time, and when possible to place it next to manure (either poultry or farm yard). I find it essential to wet the sawdust first. A mixture of equal parts wet sawdust and lawn mowings, in 1in. to 2in. thick layers, is also a good method of utilising this material.

Sea Weed.—It is only in coastal areas that direct use can be made of this valuable material, and where it can be composted, it is best to allow the surplus moisture to drain away first. Plenty of "bulk" is needed with seaweed (I have seen chopped up broccoli stumps used with good results) and my own method is to mix seaweed with an equal quantity of wet straw, and to keep the layers of this mixture as thin as pos-

15

sible, near to 3 to 4ins. in fact. When I had a garden in Somerset, a trip to the coast always meant bringing back a sack of seaweed and very valuable it proved, in the then current compost heap.

Spent Hops.—As well as being used directly in the soil, or on it as a mulch, spent hops is another useful ingredient for the gardener's compost heap. Moisten it before use and keep the layers less than 4ins. thick in the heap. As this material is light, keep it in place, if it is the top layer, with a coating of soil.

Straw.—This is often the basis of good compost. Semi-rotted or damaged straw can sometimes be purchased in country areas. Baled straw would, I feel sure, find a ready market amongst town gardeners, if an enterprising merchant or dealer gave it his attention. Straw, an activator, and water add up to a good compost, but usually the supply of straw is so small that the quantity available has to be mixed in with other materials in the compost heap. Wetted straw and poultry manure are a good combination, and where a 1 in. layer of manure can be alternated with a 3in. layer of wet straw, a very good compost is obtained.

Weeds.—Much fresh green material can be provided by the use of weeds in the compost heap. Remember, however, that if the compost is not well made and insufficient heat is obtained within the heap, some weed seeds may come through unharmed and increase the weed population considerably. To prevent trouble from weeds from the outer portions of the heap, "chip off" these areas and use the material in the centre of the current heap. Use weeds which have not yet run to seed wherever possible.

Using Farm Yard Manure, Poultry Manure, and Sewage Sludge in Compost Making.

Farm Yard Manure.—If some farm yard manure is available, make good use of it in the compost heap, where approximately one part can be used to 5 parts of the vegetable waste

Asters Ostrich Plume. For the summer bedding out displays, a range of colours are available, and for cutting also, Asters are most valuable material. I find it best to have a small oblong heap of farm yard manure, covered with a galvanised sheet to keep off rain, and to draw from this as vegetable waste becomes available. My method is to use a 2in. layer of manure alternated with a 4in. to 6in. layer of other constituents. If only a small quantity of material is available, the proportion may be as low as 1 part manure to 10 parts of other compost ingredients. If poultry manure is being used, the proportion can be approximately 1 to 20 parts.

Poultry Manure.—This is especially valuable in the compost heap. It acts as an activator by "warming up" very rapidly. I find that as little as a 1in. layer, alternated with 3 or 4in. layers of other material, works very well. Damp the manure over, if it is dry, but do not saturate it.

Sewage Sludge.—This, and other sewage manures, are available in some areas. Those in dry powder form are easiest to apply. Some types can be applied direct to the soil but all can be used in the compost heaps. 1 part sewage to 10 parts other (vegetable) compost material is suggested.

Activators, Lime, and Wood Ashes.

Activators.—One of the main needs in assisting the rotting down of material in a compost heap, and helping the work of the bacteria responsible, is nitrogen. This may be obtained by the use of chemical activators. I prefer the use of a herbal product (the Quick Return Compost Maker), which is very satisfactory. Follow the directions for use closely. The powder is first soaked in water and the mixture then poured onto the heap or into the ventilation hole. This product is a mixture of powdered herbs and other ingredients, including honey.

If you are lucky enough to have one of the animal manures to use as an "activator" this will serve the purpose admirably. Sewage sludge may also be used.

Lime.—This is needed in compost making as a neutralizer for acids and to promote conditions suitable for the bacteria which are responsible for the rotting down process. For small

17

compost heaps, comprising a variety of materials, I find that 4ozs. of hydrated lime to each square yard of heap surface, or to every barrow load of material used, gives good results.

Wood Ashes.—During the making of the heap, if wood ash is available (I like to keep some especially for the purpose), sprinkle 4ozs. to each square yard of heap surface at intervals every 15 to 18ins.

Using Compost in the Flower Garden.

If a fresh start is being made, and a plot is being prepared for a specific purpose, as for a herbaceous border, I would prefer to dig the area first. Then I should fork in as generous a layer of compost as is available, say 2ins., but 3ins. if possible, and to keep this in the top 4ins. of soil.

On established borders, fork in a similar layer each winter but avoid damage to the roots of plants in so doing. If the plants are so close that little forking is possible, leave the compost as a mulch on the surface.

If a new plot is being prepared and ample compost is available dig in about 2lbs. to the square yard, as well as forking in the dressing described above. If only one application can be given, I prefer the surface dressing, lightly forked in as already mentioned.

Flower beds can be treated in the same way as are herbaceous borders, and the forking in of a surface dressing, prior to planting, should always be aimed at. A further mulch, even if only 1in. thick, is of great benefit, also, especially in a hot dry summer.

Where surface dressings have been forked in one year, and the plot comes empty, do not dig this deeply. It can be dug a little deeper than when the compost was forked in, but only a little. Aim at improving the quality of the soil from the top down. Repeated treatment on even the heaviest soils will bring about a vast improvement in the physical structure and the "workability" of the soil, as well as increased quality of flowers and growth generally.

It may well be that the amount of compost which can be applied to the flower garden is strictly limited by the material available for the actual making. If one has vegetables and flowers, the latter may suffer to the benefit of the vegetables. The best advice that can be given is to use as much as is available, each year, paying special attention to dahlias, chrysanthemums and roses, giving moderate dressings to the herbaceous border and the bedding plants, and the least amount to the annual border sown direct.

Animal Manures and Other Organic Materials used by themselves.

I have heard of a dead horse being buried at the bottom of a new vine border and of dead cows being used similarly for fertilising purposes, but this usage of animal waste material is so rare that it is mentioned merely for interest. I once knew an enthusiastic grower of sweet peas who filled the bottom of the trenches with waste fish, with very good results. As far as whole animals are concerned, the average gardener may find the odd dead mouse, or even a dead bird, finding its way into the compost heap, but that is likely to be all, by way of animals.

Farm Yard Manure.—This may now be almost unavailable although I was surprised on several occasions last winter, in a London suburb, to be offered a load of this rare material. The price was high, however, and the quality not to my liking. If a supply is available, dig it in at 4 to 5lbs. to the square yard, for the flower garden.

Farm yard manure varies considerably, for it may be from horses, cows, pigs or mixed stock, and the bedding used may have been straw or other material. If only a small quantity irrespective of type can be obtained, for direct digging in, keep it for dahlias or chrysanthemums, which will benefit most of all from its application.

Poultry Manure.—If this is used by itself, a satisfactory rate of application for flower crops is ¼lb. to each square yard. Its manurial value varies, but a typical analysis usually shows that it is high in nitrogen.

Spent Hops.—Some gardeners are fortunate enough to live in an area where these can be obtained from a brewery. The material is extremely useful for mulching flower crops in summer or for forking into the top few inches of soil in winter. It contains varying amounts of nitrogen, often about 3 per cent, but it is for its organic rather than its nitrogenous content that it is used. For digging or forking into the soil, in winter or early spring, use a bucketful to each square yard.

Peat.—There are several grades or types and it is the granulated types that are used mostly for inclusion in potting composts. Other, finer-textured grades are available and sometimes used for mulching lawns or flowers, but these are too expensive for widespread use.

On a new soil, and before compost is available, if peat is dug in by itself it improves the organic content of the soil although it does not add much in the way of manurial material. The rate of application for digging in, on heavy soil, is a bucketful to the square yard. It is best kept in the top 6ins. of soil, to get the fullest benefit. I like to fork it in, after the first rough digging has been weathered for a few months, thus retaining it in the surface layer, rather than burying it a spade depth down.

Wood Ashes.—The chief nutrient in wood ash, is potash. Although the actual amount may be variable, many samples contain 5% potash. If the ashes are not used straight away, store them in sacks in a dry place, for, if left exposed to rain, most of their value is quickly lost. Wood ashes can be used as a base dressing for all flower crops at 2 to 3ozs. to the square yard.

Dried Blood.—This usually contains about 15% nitrogen and is quick acting. It can be used in the early stages of building up the nutrient level of a flower garden—that is until supplies of compost become available. It should be applied at 1 to 2ozs. to the square yard, between growing crops.

Bone Meal and Steamed Bone Flour.—Bone meal contains approximately 30% phosphoric acid and 3% nitrogen both of

20

which are released very slowly. For use on flower beds and borders, in the initial preparation, 4ozs. to the square yard may be applied.

Steamed bone flour is quicker acting than bone meal and contains 25 to 30% phosphoric acid and 1% nitrogen. It too can be used at 4ozs. to the square yard, as an alternative to bone meal.

Green Manures.—If one is concerned mostly with a flower garden, there may not be much space available for making use of a green crop, to dig in as manure. The most likely use of this valuable procedure, may be in a new garden, and the annual lupin is one of the most useful plants for green manuring. A small area can be sown, the seed broadcast in April or May, and the foliage stems cut down, whilst in flower, for digging in. Mustard can also be used as a green crop. Seed may be sown, broadcast at the rate of 4ozs. to 10 square yards, at any time between April and July. Dig in the stems and foliage, having first cut the mustard down, just as the flowers show. Make sure to get mustard dug in before severe frosts. Whilst digging in either lupins or mustard, add 1oz. of dried blood to each square yard, to help the rotting down process.

No Digging.

This means in practice, surface cultivations combined with the liberal use of compost to improve a soil from the top down as it were. It takes as its example, nature's own method of replacement of surface layers by leaves, rotting grass and other organic residues, and leaving the lower layers of soil as they are.

The value of a high earthworm population of soils where no digging is practised, is clear, and the object should be to increase their numbers as much as possible. My own experience of "no digging" methods has been that compost must be available in near abundance, for which reason I feel that this system should come later in the organic gardener's programme.

It is true that some aspects of flower growing, like the herbaceous border, lend themselves very well to management by surface cultivation only. It is here, I feel, that a start could be made.

I would however prefer to "build up" a soil with compost, before turning over to no digging methods. It must be borne in mind that a 2in. layer of compost will be needed each winter, if this method is to be adopted.

It would not be wise to try "no digging" on hard, heavy soil, that had not been cultivated at all, or not for some time. Normal digging should be done for at least two seasons, I feel, before trying a bed or border to flower crops. As well as the herbaceous border already mentioned, annuals or bedding plants could be tried under this method.

If perennial weeds are present, every effort must be made to remove these, by digging out the roots, before a plot is switched over to no digging methods. This applies to docks, convolvulus, ground elder and buttercup, in particular.

If an area is turned over to "no digging" methods, a 2in. layer of compost should be applied and raked over to remove any large pieces, in spring, prior to seeds being sown (as in an annual border). If seeds can be covered with a further dressing of compost, of appropriate depth, so much the better.

Remember that weed seeds will find a compost surface very attractive. Close attention may be needed to their removal on a plot where no digging is done and the compost surface is maintained.

If an existing herbaceous border is turned over to no digging methods it is best, for the first season, at least to loosen the soil between the clumps, before applying the recommended 2ins. of compost in autumn or spring.

As most herbaceous plants have to be lifted every few years, to prevent overcrowding and subsequent weakening of growth, this in itself ensures much of the soil being stirred. It is well worth setting aside a portion of the border at least, which is not to be dug for 3 or 4 seasons and to rely on surface applications of compost.

With herbaceous plants in particular, there will be a considerable amount of fresh roots made, into the compost layers, this being especially apparent after the second year. When this takes place, deep cultivation would damage this fresh and active root system.

To summarise, it is best to try some "no digging" on a small scale first, to gain experience and note results. If the response under one's own conditions justifies it, the undug area may be extended.

Proprietary Organic Manures.

When a new flower garden is being made, there may be very little compost-making material available, and a small quantity of a proprietary product may need to be purchased. Cost may preclude more than a small amount being used but the choice of materials is fairly wide.

There is a new product available at present, made from grape pips and waste grape material. It is used at the rate of 1lb. to each square yard.

There are several proprietary organic manures based on spent hops and these may be considered for use in the initial stages as may those based on seaweed. Various fish compounds are also available. Mention should be made of several meat and bone, or blood, meat and bone preparations.

When considering costs with these preparations, I am thinking of the price in relation to their being used as the sole means of providing organic matter.

Mention is made frequently to these and similar organic products being used in conjunction with compost with special reference to individual crops.

Chapter II

Planning and Layout.

1. Some General Points.

2. Some Soil Cultivations.

3. Initial Work and Planning. Herbaceous Borders. Lawns. Flower Borders and Beds. The New Rock Garden.

4. Planning for Seasonal Display.

5. Keeping down costs.

6. Some plants for a Shaded Border.

Some General Points.

It may well be that your garden is already laid out, and no major re-organisation is necessary, but if you are starting with a new garden, the following points may be considered.

1. Lawns. It is usual to have the lawn in front of the house, with flowers around it and, possibly, depending on the size, flower beds of varying shapes within the lawn. Often one can plan for another grass area behind the house, especially if children are being considered. Grass seed for areas of the latter type can be less expensive than for the main lawn and the mixture for harder wear, may contain some rye grass. Try to avoid too small a patch of lawn. It is best to economise on the borders rather than the grass area. Narrow flower borders go well with a lawn, but grow subjects of suitable height to match the width.

2. The herbaceous border may be large or small (general guidance is given later), but avoid crowding plants together if space is limited. If only a small narrow border can be planned for, use the dwarfer growing plants. Try to choose a position where the plants will be seen to the best advantage. If a grass verge is possible, the front edge need not be straight; curves give the impression of a greater "sweep" of colour.

3. Flower beds should, if possible be so arranged that they can be seen from the house. Often, other people get the best view of a display!

4. Avoid too many small flower beds, as these mean more work in trimming edges and general maintenance. One bold display is better than several small beds in most cases.

5. Plan to have an extra area where flowers can be grown for cutting only. This means that the herbaceous border, grown for decoration, does not get "robbed" unduly by cutting blooms for indoor display.

6. An area will also be needed for keeping some plants in reserve, for propagation, seed sowing or growing plants on, and to lay in bulbs and other plants temporarily. Such an area may well be in use for most of the year, for one or other of these purposes.

26

Some Soil Cultivations.

Digging.—In addition to a spade, a broad tined fork (see Fig. 2) is useful for this work on heavy soil. Never dig a heavy clay soil when it is wet, or it will "set" and be very hard to break down. There is little point in digging a light soil in early winter, as the rain will only leach much of the organic matter away, but a heavy soil should be dug as early as possible in autumn (delaying compost application until spring) so as to obtain the maximum weathering effect from wind, rain, frost and snow.

Fig. 2.—Digging Fork

If one has much digging to do, tackle only a little at a time to avoid the job becoming too laborious. Digging in short spells, say 15 minutes, and going on to another job for 10 minutes is a useful practice. When digging use the full depth of the spade or fork. Leave the surface as rough as possible when digging in autumn or winter, this being especially applicable on a newly cultivated area, where soil is very heavy.

Forking.—If the soil between established herbaceous

27

plants is being forked over, use a fork with short tines as this makes the job much easier where many roots come near to the surface.

Hoeing.—For working between narrow rows of small seedlings a short handled "onion" hoe is best (see Fig 3), as this allows for close manipulation. It is also useful for hoeing between young flower plants as in a flower bed, or between bedding plants not long planted.

Where one has more room to work, choose a long handled hoe, either of the Dutch type (see Fig. 4), which one walks backwards to use, or the Draw hoe, which one walks forward to utilise. In either case, keep the blade of the hoe sharp, filing it occasionally to keep a good "edge", as this makes for much easier work.

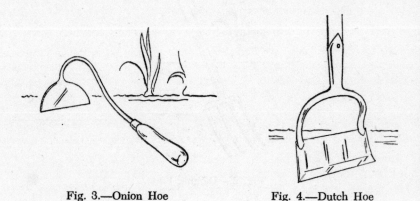

Fig. 3.—Onion Hoe   Fig. 4.—Dutch Hoe

As a basic principle, remember that if hoeing is done before any weeds show, little weed growth will develop. Soil disturbance kills many germinating weed seeds below surface level.

Cultivation, for Sowing or Planting.

When preparing a flower bed for planting or sowing, the forking in of a layer of compost will considerably improve

28

both texture and workability. To obtain the final tilth, for sowing especially, use a wooden rake first, then an iron rake. In working down a heavy soil, try to "catch" the lumps after a shower of rain, or if water can be applied use this to soften them. A light roller is a good piece of equipment at this stage, otherwise, in the early stages of cultivation on a heavy soil, the surface may have to be worked down by beating it with the back of a spade, to break the lumps.

Other Cultivations.—One of the most useful tools for the flower garden, is a 3 or 5-prong hand cultivator (see Fig. 5). This is used for breaking down soil to be sown or planted, or for inter-row cultivation, or for stirring the soil between growing plants. Regular use of this tool prevents the soil from

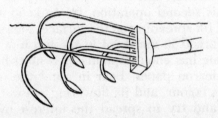

Fig. 5.—Cultivator

cracking and thus helps to retain moisture. The easiest method of using this tool is to draw it toward one, whilst walking backwards slowly. Avoid using a cultivator too close to growing plants or damage will be caused to the roots and the plants will be loosened.

Initial Work and Planning.

(a.) *Herbaceous Borders.*
Some practical points to consider in the early stages are:—
1. A grass verge gives a good contrast to herbaceous plants, but the border may have to be alongside a path, in which case avoid having tall or very spreading subjects nearest to the path itself.

29

2. Bear in mind the season of flowering, i.e., plan for a long season of flower, or a late display, or perhaps with a bias toward favourite colours.

3. If the border is very narrow, avoid having too tall a choice of subjects at the back. Many of the larger subjects reach 6ft. in height and ample width is needed to be able to include these plants.

4. Take every opportunity to remove perennial weed roots when the initial digging is being done. These weeds, such as convolvulus, thistle, dock and buttercup, can be extremely difficult to deal with once herbaceous plants become established.

5. Remember that the border will stay down for some years and that no deep cultivation will be possible after planting. Dig the plot as deeply as practicable and, later, fork or dig it through again to keep the soil in its original level.

6. After this second operation, try to keep a 2in. layer of compost for spreading on the surface. This should be very lightly forked in and kept in the top few inches of soil.

7. When one has enough plants, it is most helpful to plan the border on paper. Bear in mind the height of each plant, its colour, and its flowering season. Avoid colour clashes and try to spread the interest over the whole border for as long a period as possible.

8. It is helpful to remember that plants of short or medium height (2 to 2½ft.) require little or no staking, which means less labour subsequently.

9. If in any doubt as to choice of subjects, all those described in Chapter 8 can be relied upon. For further choice it is always helpful to make a note of any that catch the eye during summer and plan to include some of these later, as room allows.

(b.) *Lawns.*

A well kept lawn or other grass area shows off flowers to the best advantage whereas a poor lawn can detract considerably from flower borders and beds nearby. If one is starting with a new garden, this gives a good opportunity of obtaining a first-class lawn. Remembering that a lawn should stay down for many years, give as deep a digging by way of initial preparation, as is possible. This does not mean bringing up unweathered sub-soil to the surface, but try to dig deeply, to the full depth of the spade in the first place. If sufficient compost is available, fork a 1 to 2in. layer into the top 3ins. of soil, then fork shallowly through the whole area again.

The first digging is best done in autumn or winter, to allow for the maximum weathering effect. Grass seed is sown in March or April, or if this is not possible, in late August or early September. In either case after forking through the dug plot, to add the compost, use a wooden rake, then an iron rake to get as good a depth of workable soil on top (tilth) as is possible. Level the plot as this work proceeds. Also apply a dressing of bone meal, at 3ozs. per square yard, during the raking operations. If it is possible to allow a batch of annual weeds to develop before sowing, so much the better. If two crops can be allowed to grow, and be hoed off, this is better still.

The soil must be in the right state for sowing, i.e. not so wet that it "sticks" to the boots. Rake over the bed, finally, and mark it off with strings into yard wide strips. Allow 1½ozs. of seeds mixture to each square yard which, if the plot is, say, 6 yards long, means 9ozs. of grass seed for each strip. Weigh off the required number of 9ozs., so that an even distribution can be obtained. Lay some wide planks on the strip alongside the one to be sown, and sow the seed evenly, if possible at a time when rain threatens. There should be little wind, or sowing is made difficult.

Rake the seed in very lightly to reduce loss by birds, and roll the sown strip if the surface is very loose and puffy. This may not be necessary on heavy soils. Manipulate the roller from the planks, which should be moved over afterwards, the strip on which they were lying raked over, and the process repeated.

A good quality grass seed mixture contains no rye grass; the following is ideal: 7 parts Chewings Fescue and 3 parts New Zealand Brown Top. The extra cost is well worth while, as a good quality lawn will be obtained, where cutting will not have to be done so frequently as if a rye grass mixture is used.

(c.) *Flower Borders and Beds.*

Some general guidance on annual borders which are sown

direct and on flower beds is given in Chapter 3. For the most part, annual flowers are shallow rooted and do not require the same depth of cultivation as the stronger growing, deeper rooted herbaceous plants. However, the beds or borders should be dug to the depth of the spade and as much compost as can be spared be dug in. A 2in. layer of compost, forked lightly into the top 3ins. of soil, will be of special benefit. Prior to planting or sowing, add 2ozs. of bone meal to the square yard, and rake this into the top few inches also.

Some Spring Bedding Schemes.—When planning ahead, wallflowers are often a first choice, but they are sometimes combined with daffodils. The dark red varieties of wallflowers go well with a large trumpet variety of daffodil, such as Rembrandt. Myosotis is often used as an "under crop" for both daffodils and tulips, the blue "base" providing an effective contrast for pink and yellow tulips in particular. Sweet Williams give a late display and can best be followed with bedding dahlias, as these are one of the latest subjects that can be planted.

For a spring display with a difference try a "mixed" bed. If you have some plants of polyanthus, pansies, red and white double daisies, myosotis, or Siberian wallflowers, plant them in a mixed bed, at a spacing of 8ins. The resulting effect will be bold and striking.

Some Summer Bedding Schemes.—There are many combinations that can be planned for, using the subjects described in Chapter 8, and individual choice and preference can be given full rein. Some of the more popular combinations are scarlet geraniums and blue lobelia, pink antirrhinums and lobelia or alyssum edging. Remember that mixed colours of the same subject, like stocks, asters, or nemesia, make a bold display. Often one can use a dwarfer form of the same subject as an edging, e.g., antirrhinums or nemesia.

If there are several flower beds, the colours may be the same in each bed, but each bed a different shade. Contrasting coloured edging plants, e.g. ageratum, mesembryanthemum, lobelia, or alyssum, make for a wider appeal, and some beds can have more than one type of edging plant to give contrast.

The Herbaceous Border. Whether large or small, such a border provides colour and interest over many months

In general, plan for bold displays, making full use of one's favourite colours, and aim at "ringing the changes" from year to year.

(e.) *The New Rock Garden.*

Where a new rock garden is being planned for, choose a site that is not shaded and avoid especially one which is under trees, as the damp conditions which result will be detrimental to many rock plants. A position in full sun is best, and one which is sheltered from cold winds.

Ease of access is another important point, and the rock garden may adjoin the lawn, or a hard path, so that it can easily receive attention. A small easy-to-manage rockery is best, at least to begin with. If this can be planned so that extension can take place, if desired, so much the better.

Where some new stone is purchased, or if an existing rock garden is being renovated, it is a good practice to bury ¾ of the total amount of stone or rock used, so that only ¼ is in evidence above soil level. Limestone, or red sandstone, give a pleasing effect. Rock or stone should be laid in the front of a new plot, and set to slope slightly backwards. Work up from this first layer, setting subsequent rocks behind the first. Avoid a fixed step arrangement; try to obtain a finished appearance such that the stone appears to be jutting out of the soil, in natural strata (layers).

In planning the situations for various subjects, try to obtain flowers in all parts of the rock garden over a long period. Aim at having something in flower for as much of the year as possible. Do not have all the spring flowering subjects in the same area, or this will be a "blank" for the rest of the season.

Often one has to ensure that the soil for many rock plants is not too rich, or growth will be too strong, and unmanageable. A shallow depth of soil and compost, in equal parts, in pockets, or a shallow pocket of soil with but surface dressings of compost, is a good general guide.

Plants which prefer dry conditions and make a rosette of leaves or which resent dampness around them, will do best if a layer of gravel chippings, ½in. thick, is laid around and between them. Many of the Saxifrages are examples in this category.

33

Most rock plants need to be planted fairly firmly. The usual planting season is in autumn but spring planting is also satisfactory. Most rock plants are sold in pots, in any case, so that there is less difficulty in deciding when to plant.

Planning for Seasonal Displays.

Various types of flower displays can be made up of:

      Annual Borders.
      Bedding Plants (Spring).
      Bedding Plants (Summer).
      Bulbs and Corms.
      Herbaceous Borders.

As far as the actual display is concerned, Annual Borders, that is where one sows the seed direct where plants are to flower, give colour from June to September, with the peak in July and August. Spring bedding plants provide colour in April and May; Summer bedding in June, July and August, with the latest subjects like bedding dahlias continuing until September. Bulbs and corms provide spring and summer flowers, whilst the herbaceous border, with careful planning, can give plants in flower from April to September with, usually, a peak in July. It may not be possible to plan for all of these types of display, and one may even have to compromise, and have a mixed border, that is, one made up of herbaceous plants, and spring and summer bedding plants, with a few bulbs as well.

Keeping Down Costs.

There are several factors that can be borne in mind, which help to provide an inexpensive display of flowers. The cheapest form of flower border is made with the annuals which can be sown direct where they are to flower. Full details are given in Chapter 3.

Raising one's own bedding plants as described in Chapter 7 is also a means of economising, as is the production of summer bedding plants, or even some of them, where one has a heated green house. Many herbaceous perennials can be raised from seed, as described in Chapter 3, and fullest possible use should be made of this aspect, especially if one is starting with a new garden, as there are many suitable subjects.

Remember that the newer the variety, the dearer it is to buy. If herbaceous plants are being purchased, select the more common, less expensive sorts to begin with. Another method of saving money is to buy a nucleus of herbaceous plants in autumn, plant them up in a border or plot by themselves, grow them on for one year, or even two, then divide them, thus obtaining two, three, or more times the original number. This delays the planting of the herbaceous border proper but, in the meantime, the area concerned can be sown with annuals, or utilised for bedding plants.

If only a few plants are purchased, another method of economy is to plant them at twice the normal distance apart, to allow for their being lifted and divided later. For the first season the gaps can be planted with bedding plants, or annuals.

If one can obtain a few plants here and there, from friends, so much the better, but I am assuming that few may be available from such sources and that the garden has to be entirely stocked out of one's own pocket.

Seed can be saved from many annual flowers, especially the hardy subjects sown direct. This is especially applicable where a batch of mixed colours of the same subject is being grown. In general one should save seed from the best plants. Pick off the seed pods or seed heads under dry conditions, and finish ripening off in a dry, cool, airy place. When the seed can be shaken out readily, store this too, under similar conditions, in suitably sized packets, making sure that each variety is labelled.

Some Plants for a Shaded Border.

Where one has to deal with a shaded position, the choice of plants is rather restricted. A selection of suitable subjects which can be grown under these conditions could include some of the following:

For spring flowering, Polyanthus, in mixed colours can be given pride of place. Do not leave the plants too long before dividing them; if possible split up a few crowns each year after flowering. Give a 1in. layer of compost, or leaf mould, between the plants each spring for best quality flowers.

Forget-me-nots are another subject for a shaded plot but need to be planted each year, for best results. Their blue flowers blend well with narcissi and daffodils, which give quite a good effect in a similar position.

Lily of the Valley can also be included, but make every effort to place a mulch of compost at least 1in. thick over the crowns in early spring.

A few plants of violets can also be included on the shaded border. This is another plant that thrives where there is ample compost in the top few inches of soil.

To turn to herbaceous plants, Aquilegas are useful where the border does not get very much sunshine. They provide useful colour in May and June. The new hybrid varieties now available are a considerable improvement on the older types.

Another useful plant for shade, although taller than many, being about 5ft. high, is the Digitalis or Foxglove. The Mertenensis variety is shorter however, being 2½ft. high and a pleasing strawberry colour. Like their hedgerow cousins, which revel in a soil containing humus and leaf mould, the garden varieties should have a generous dressing of compost worked into the top few inches of soil before planting. Many Digitalis are biennials, and seed should be sown each year in May or June to give plants for flowering the following season.

Anemone Japonica does equally well in sun or shade, and seems to thrive under most soil conditions. Once well established it should be left alone. The red variety Anemone Japonica Rubra is very attractive for September and October flowering.

A gem of a plant for the semi-shaded border is the Tibetan Poppy *Meconopsis betonicifolia*, var. *Baileyii*. Plants are raised from seed sown as soon as ripe in early autumn. The planting site should have a generous dressing of compost and leaf mould in equal parts, worked into the top 3ins. of soil, and the plants be given a mulch each spring of equal parts of coarse grit and leaf mould. The sky blue flowers in July, are in a class apart. Do not allow the flowers to develop until more than one rosette of leaves has formed. Although the foliage is rather large, a useful spring flowering subject for a shaded

36

position, is *Bergenia cordifolia*. The variety *purpurea*, which is carmine purple, and 2ft. high, can be recommended.

Pulmonaria is another shade-loving plant, which flowers in the spring. It does well on most soils and the variety P. Montana is useful, with its bright salmon red flowers in March and April. It grows 15ins. high.

Paeonies are a must for the shaded border where their bold, colourful blooms in June and July are an asset. They are dealt with in more detail in Chapter 8.

Chapter III

Flower Garden Management

Summary of the main operations involving
Annual Borders, Bedding Plants (Spring
and Summer), Herbaceous Borders, Lawns
and Rock Gardens throughout the year.

JANUARY.

General.—This is the quiet month as far as outdoor work is concerned, and every opportunity should be taken to re-plan borders, decide on bedding schemes, and order the necessary seeds, after a careful study of the new catalogues. It is a good plan to obtain catalogues from several different seedsmen, as all contain some illustrations, many in colour, and full use should be made of these in planning the layout and colour schemes in annual borders.

Spring Bedding Plants.—After very hard frosts, some of these plants, such as wallflowers, may become loosened, and should be re-firmed if necessary. Polyanthus may be showing some brown or dead foliage which should be picked off and composted. If at this stage, some leaf mould is available, spread a 1in. layer over the soil between these plants, as they benefit considerably from this treatment.

FEBRUARY.

General.—When flower seeds have been purchased, and each plot or bed is to be labelled (this always makes the flower garden more interesting), the labels can be written now. Painted wooden labels are suitable, and the necessary writing (printing is best) should be done with a thick black garden pencil. Herbaceous plants can have a label also; those 8ins. long are suitable and can be inscribed in readiness for any new varieties not yet planted or for existing plants.

MARCH.

Herbaceous Border.—If you are re-planting, or if any new planting is not yet completed, try to get this done by the end of the month. With any such later work, pay particular attention to watering if the weather should be dry in the following weeks.

Although normally done in the autumn, it is still not too late for division of overgrown plants but, again, do not delay

40

this work longer than necessary. Should the soil be sufficiently wet, however, early April is not too late for re-planting.

Lawns, Trimming the Edges.—The edge or verge of the lawn should be kept neat by cutting a small slice off with a half moon or edging knife. If the edge is straight, use a line stretched tightly to ensure tidy work, or, for a small area, use a plank laid flat against the edge concerned, and work from this. The grass can be kept neat at the edges later with a hand shears, or a special type of long-handled shears for the purpose.

The Rock Garden.—An important point at this time of year is to see that dead leaves are not allowed to accumulate. If some are blown on to the rock garden and allowed to lie around low-growing plants, which do not like damp conditions, damage may result.

Remove any such leaves regularly, as damp conditions can also lead to slugs being active. If any plants are being damaged, it may be necessary to put down some slug baits, especially if the weather is mild. Such material should be placed in flower pots standing on their sides, so that it remains dry, and more effective over a long period.

If any plants have been lost, or severely damaged by hard weather, take note of gaps that require to be filled, so that replacements can be planned.

Where the surface soil has become hard or set, as a result of wintry weather, stir the top inch with a small hand cultivator. This makes for better aeration and better growth when roots become active again. Should any weeds remain, pull these out at the same time. Take the opportunity also, of renewing any gravel chippings that may be needed around the crowns of plants which benefit from this treatment—such as saxifrages and other plants with low-growing foliage.

If birds are troublesome at this time of year, and start to damage polyanthus buds, or other spring flowers, try placing some small, coloured plastic windmills near the plants concerned. Small red, or other brightly-coloured flags, are often effective. Sometimes stringing black cotton over the plants is the best method of preventing bird damage.

41

APRIL.

Annual Borders.—A very colourful display of summer and early autumn flowers can be obtained, at reasonable cost, by setting aside a border or some of the flower beds for selected annuals which can be sown directly where they are to flower. The longer the border the bolder the effect, yet even a small area can be utilised for this type of bedding or border display. Fuller details of the subjects which one can use for this purpose are given in Chapter 8.

The plot to be used for these annuals can be sown this month. When the soil is dry and easily worked, use a wooden rake to obtain a fine depth. Then, draw drills with a small hand hoe or even with the point of a dibber, 6ins. apart for dwarf subjects up to 9ins. high, 9ins. apart for plants 9ins. to 18ins., and 12ins. apart for taller specimens. Mark out the area into patches of about a square foot, and bear in mind that the drills need not all be the same way.

The depth of the drills should be such that the seeds will have ½in. of soil over them. Sow the seeds thinly, 1 to 3 to every inch of drill. Cover in the rows with an iron rake and firm down the soil with the back of a rake. Afterwards, rake over the plot, lightly. Set small wooden labels in each section, or in the plots containing subjects which one does not know, or which one has not grown before.

If a border backing on to a wall or fence is being used, keep the taller subjects at the back. If planting onto a bed, use tall varieties in the centre and shorter subjects on either side.

In about 7 to 10 days some of the seedlings will be showing. It is then best to hoe between the rows, as soon as they can be seen.

The seedlings should be thinned out when large enough to handle. On average 4 to 5ins. spacing for the dwarf subjects and 6 to 7ins. for the rest, will serve very well for ordinary display. Always leave the best plants when thinning and, if possible, do the work in dull, damp weather, or when rain threatens.

Bedding Plants, Spring.—When the early subjects go out of flower, i.e. wallflowers, double daisies and polyanthus, clear

42

the plants for compost making. Remember that the best poly-anthus can be divided if increase is needed.

Herbaceous Borders.—This is a busy month for herbaceous plants. Hoeing should not be neglected, and a feed of 2ozs. of bone meal to the square yard will be of benefit, if the compost dressing was not as heavy as one would like. Staking is important and tall subjects such as Helianthus, Delphiniums and Solidago, should have canes pushed in, in threes, or fours, with the shoots kept within bounds by looping fillis string around the canes at half the height of the plants and again at three quarters of the potential height. Plants 2 to 3ft. in height can have tall sticks pushed in around and between them. The sticks should be slightly shorter than the height the plants normally reach. Whether canes or sticks are used, push them in firmly. Start staking when plants are about half their full height.

Shorter plants need staking with some bushy twigs as supports. Such material should be placed in position when the plants are half grown. Hoe between the plants for as long as possible, that is, until they touch across the rows.

Lawns.—Rolling should not be overdone but is often necessary to give firm conditions. It makes for a better level and consequently easier mowing. Do not use a heavy roller when the soil is very wet or it will set so hard on the surface that poor aeration results and moss will very probably be encouraged.

Mowing.—Mowing should start this month and continue regularly from now on, unless very hot weather causes so little growth that mowing is delayed. Any very coarse grasses which escape the mower should be cut off with shears. Often, mowing in a different direction will cut off some of these tough growths.

Under dry conditions, it is best not to use the grass box. Allow the mowings to fall on the lawn and stay there, to add organic matter as they rot in. This is good practice to follow for one mowing in three at other times, also, particularly on a lawn where it is known the soil is not of high organic content.

Never cut the grass too short; aim at a ¾in. "cover" above ground level, which will be springy, tough, and wear resistant.

Wormcasts.—Wormcasts can be dealt with by brushing them level with a flexible "besom" type broom, as often as they appear. Avoid leaving the casts undisturbed, or they will give the lawn a muddy surface after wet weather.

Lawns.—If it is known that the soil is poor, apply a dressing of the following mixture, at the rate of 2ozs. to the square yard:

2 parts bone flour, 1 part hoof and horn and 1 part wood ashes. This is best applied in damp weather or when rain threatens. It should not be necessary if a generous amount of compost was worked into the surface prior to sowing but may be needed on a neglected lawn.

MAY.

Annual Borders.—As the plants grow away after thinning, hoe them through once, or more, until they fill up the space available and thus smother further weed growth. Any large weeds that show up later can be thinned out by hand, but take care not to loosen the flower plants when this is done.

Most annuals are self supporting, but taller subjects such as lavatera, cornflower and larkspur, can have a few pieces of bushy, twiggy material, about 2ft. tall, inserted amongst them for extra support. The sticks should be placed in position when the plants are 9 to 10ins. high.

Bedding Plants, Summer.—About the middle of the month when planting out bedding subjects from boxes, either those raised oneself or bought in, an easy way to get the plants out of the boxes is to take one of the sides off, and to slide out the whole of the soil and plants in one piece. Individual plants can then be broken out in squares, with soil intact around the roots. Plant firmly, taking out holes with a trowel, and water the plants in after planting. As a general guide, dwarf varieties up to 6ins. high can be planted 4ins. apart, subjects 6 to 12ins.

high can be set out 6 to 8ins. apart and taller plants can be spaced at 8 to 9ins. Do not plant out the more tender subjects, such as zinnias, bedding dahlias and salvias, until early next month.

For choice of subjects, details given in Chapter 8 should be studied. Remember that in borders or beds the shorter subjects should be kept in the front, e.g., alyssum, lobelia and ageratum. Aim at contrasting colours when making up the scheme for bedding display. A bed of mixed colours of the same subject is very colourful, e.g., antirrhinums, asters, stocks, bedding dahlias or nemesia.

After planting, hoe through between the plants, once or twice, to keep down weeds and prevent the soil from cracking—which causes undue loss of moisture. A soil which has had a 2in. layer of rotted compost worked into the top few inches of soil will not crack or dry out so readily as one which is not treated.

Herbaceous Borders.—If there should be any gaps or blanks these can be filled up with hardy annuals, sown direct. Any of those described in Chapter 8 can be used. As an alternative, summer bedding plants can be utilised for any spare spaces. Such a border may not then be, strictly speaking, a "herbaceous" border, but a "mixed" border. The effect will in any case be more pleasing than if gaps and blanks were left.

Herbaceous Border, Thinning Surplus Shoots.—If the shoots of some of the stronger growing plants, such as delphiniums, are reduced to 4 or 5 to each plant, better spikes will result. Subjects like alstomeria and phlox, can be reduced to 6 shoots to each plant, and chrysanthemum maximum, Michaelmas daisy and lupins, to 6 to 8 shoots. Do not thin pyrethrum, anemone japonica, gaillardia, geum, kniphofia, or paeony. Remove the unwanted shoots completely, when small, and leave the best ones to flower.

JUNE.

Bedding Plants.—Early this month, the more tender subjects such as bedding dahlias, salvias, and zinnias, may be

45

planted out. If in boxes or borders, dahlias and salvias can be planted 9ins. apart, but zinnias need 12 to 15ins., unless the very dwarf varieties are being grown. Try to give these plants a sunny, sheltered position where they will thrive best.

The plants of other varieties set out last month should be hoed through lightly, or the soil shallowly cultivated with a 3 or 5 prong cultivator. Take care not to loosen the plants.

Bedding Plants for Next Year.—To prepare for displays of wallflowers, myosotis, double daisies and sweet williams next spring, seed may be sown now. Sow thinly and transplant the seedlings to a spare piece of ground, allowing 6ins. by 6ins. of space. Better plants will result if this can be done; if not, thin the seedlings so that they are not overcrowded in the seed bed, i.e. leave them 3 to 4ins. apart.

Raising perennial plants from seed.—Some of the plants grown in herbaceous borders may be raised from seed, the most common examples being lupins, delphiniums, aquilega and pyrethrum. Sow the seeds thinly and water the open drills prior to sowing to promote germination. Transplant seedlings 6ins. by 6ins. on a spare plot, as soon as they can be handled, after first watering in a surface dressing of compost. Plants stay in this position until autumn, or next spring, when they are planted out in flowering positions.

Mulching the Flower Borders.—Lawn mowings are a most valuable material for mulching and may be used on the herbaceous border, the annual border or between bedding plants. They have many virtues, one of which is as an aid to moisture retention. A layer of mowings also breaks the direct sun rays in a very hot spell and prevents loss of surface moisture. If watering is done in warm weather, and a mulch can follow, so much the better, as the moisture is retained for a longer period.

Do not apply too thick a layer of lawn mowings at one time; 1in. depth is ample. If a border is devoted to dahlias, or chrysanthemums, both these plants derive benefit from such a mulch. Mowings can be used fresh, i.e. applied as soon as they are cut. Any that are not wanted immediately should go

46

directly into the compost heap, in which they serve to warm up the heap and hasten the rotting down of other material used. Continue mulching into July and August.

Herbaceous Borders.—If Iris clumps have been in position for several years, they should now be lifted and the youngest portions re-planted. The new site should have some old mortar rubble mixed in with the top few inches of soil and also be given a generous dressing of compost.

The Rock Garden.—As the early flowering subjects finish flowering, the old flower heads and stalks should be cut off so that new growth can be made and next year's flowers built up, as a result. In any case, the general appearance and freshness of the rock garden display will be much improved by regular attention to this feature.

JULY.

Bedding Plants.—As the earlier flowering subjects such as antirrhinums and nemesia go over, cut off the old flower stalks so that a second flush of bloom will be encouraged. At this stage, a mulch of lawn mowings, or if available a 1in. layer of compost, will be of considerable benefit, especially if the weather is hot and dry.

Herbaceous Borders.—As the flowers go over, remove the spent blooms, both to encourage further display and to keep the appearance of the border as fresh as possible. Use the old flower heads in the compost heap as they are gathered. Make sure that the taller subjects are tied securely.

AUGUST.

Rock Garden.—There are many rock plants which can be increased from cuttings, using the new shoots, which lend themselves to propagation this month. Amongst these are phlox, aubretia, armeria, and dianthus. Unflowered shoots make the best cuttings and should be taken 2 to 3ins. long and have the lower leaves removed and the base trimmed neatly through a leaf joint with a sharp knife. Insert the cuttings firmly in small pots, about 1in. apart, in a mixture of half sand and half peat or sieved compost. Stand the pots in a cold, shaded frame, and water with care. When the cuttings are rooted, they can be potted singly into 2½in. pots in a mixture of 2 parts loam, 1 of sand and 1 of compost, and stood out in a sheltered corner until spring when they can be planted up where there is space for them.

SEPTEMBER.

Annual Border.—Before the plants are pulled up and composted, some may have set seed. If this is well ripened, a small amount from selected subjects can be saved for use next year. If the seed is ripe in pods or other seed containers, on the plant, shake some on to a newspaper and, after storage for a week or two in a dry place, place it in envelopes and store in cool dry conditions.

Bedding Plants.—As the main display finishes, and plans are being made for autumn planting, pull out the plants a bed at a time if possible, so that the material may be composted in small batches. The taller plants can be chopped up into pieces 6ins. or so long for easier handling. Try to compost whilst the foliage and stems are still green. Pull up the plants, and use roots, stems and leaves for compost making.

Planting Biennials for Spring Flowering.—As the beds or borders of annuals and bedding subjects go out of flower, pull out the plants and fork through the soil to prepare for spring bedding schemes. Suitable subjects are polyanthus, wallflowers and pansies, double daisies and sweet williams. A novel effect can be obtained by planting several of these subjects in a truly mixed bed. Planting distances, whether in a mixed or single subject scheme, can be 8ins. Make sure that the soil is firm before planting.

If a 2in. layer of compost can be spared, spread this on the forked up surface and work it into the top 3ins. of soil with the tips of a fork. Work in 3ozs. of wood ashes and 2ozs. of bone meal to each square yard, also, especially if only a small amount of compost is available.

48

Chrysanthemums. For late summer and early autumn flowering out of doors, and winter flowering in a greenhouse, chrysanthemums are without equal

Lawns.—As making a new lawn from seed and turf is dealt with, a further method should be borne in mind. This is the planting of the roots of a type of agrostis (stolonifera), in the autumn or winter. The roots can be purchased in amounts sufficient for 100 sq. ft. This grass gives a dark green lawn that requires less cutting than grass, but which is more expensive than seed. Further details should be obtained from the suppliers as space precludes more than a mention here.

The Rock Garden.—All spent flowers and stalks should be cut off, and used for composting. No plant debris or fallen leaves should be allowed to lie between the rosettes of rock plant foliage, or this may lead to damp conditions.

This is a good time to cut back any very strong-growing plants; small shears can be used for this purpose. Make sure that none of the weaker-growing plants are being smothered by their stronger-growing neighbours.

OCTOBER.

Transplant herbaceous plants raised from seed.—Plants raised as described under June work can be put out in gaps in the border or used to help fill a new border. Plant in clumps of 3 if possible, the plants set at 9 to 12ins. apart, depending on their ultimate height. Plant firmly, using a trowel, lifting the plants with as much soil around the roots as possible. Do not plant if the soil is very wet; if needs be, planting can be delayed until the spring.

Herbaceous Borders.—If the border is not unduly exposed the old spent stems and foliage should be cut down to the level of the crowns. First, though, pull out the canes and pea stick material, and store this away in a dry place, for further use, if still sound enough.

When all the cleaning up is completed, spread a 2in. layer of rotted compost on the soil between the plants, and lightly fork this in so that it is mixed with the top 3ins. of soil.

Many subjects can be lifted and split into smaller crowns every second year, e.g. michaelmas daisies, chrysanthemum

C F G—4

maximum, and erigeron, thus preventing overcrowding with these rather prolific subjects (see Fig. 6).

It is an easy matter to increase most perennials by root division. It should be attended to annually, in order to prevent the flowers from becoming smaller and smaller. If the clump of root is large and firmly interlaced (pyrethrums and michaelmas daisies are familiar types), the simplest way is to place a couple of garden forks right through the root clump, back to back. Then pull the inter-growing roots apart by a steady leverage. If it is unnecessary to use the bulk of root, pull out

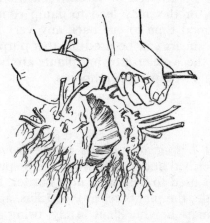

Fig. 6.—Method for dividing clumps of herbaceous plants

a few of the strongest shoots, with roots attached, from the outside of the clump and replant. The shoots at the centre of the clump are the old exhausted original plant, and should be thrown away. Small plants such as forget-me-nots and polyanthus, may be divided by means of a trowel, or by pulling apart with the fingers.

Lawns.—One of the most useful tools for lawn maintenance is a springbok rake. This can be used to rake out moss and dead grass, which treatment gives the remaining grass a much better chance to make fresh growth. Two or more rakings may be needed at this time of year. Remember that all such material raked up makes an ideal ingredient for the compost heap, and every scrap should be utilised.

The use of this tool promotes better surface aeration and, as a result, better root action.

Lawns, Laying Turf.—If it is convenient to buy in sufficient turf for a small lawn this may be laid now or during the next few weeks. Turf laid in the autumn has the longest possible period in which to "knit". The soil preparation should be as for seed sowing but, immediately before laying the turf, roll the area to get it quite level and firm. Turf is usually in pieces 3ft. by 1ft., and should be laid so that the "joins" in each row, do not come opposite each other. Firm the turf in position by laying a plank down, flat, and standing on it. When all the turf is laid, scatter some fine soil and compost, equal parts of each, into the cracks, and roll the area to settle the turf into position. It is best to avoid using the new lawn for a few weeks if possible.

By comparison with seed sowing, turf is more expensive, but it has the advantage of giving a usable area more quickly. Buy only good quality, weed free, turf for best results.

NOVEMBER.

Lawns.—Aeration in a lawn is all important and this can be obtained by "spiking" with a fork. A special hollow-tined fork can be used for this purpose. There are also small rollers with spikes attached which can be pushed over the lawn to make numerous holes that serve to give better aeration. On a small area, a fork may be used, and it is best to treat a strip at a time, driving the tines in to their full depth, at intervals of 4 to 6ins. each way. Move the tines to and fro before pulling them out. Peat or ashes can be brushed into the holes, thus improving both drainage and the air supply to the soil; even better results will be obtained from a mixture of 3 parts soil, 1 of compost and 1 of sand. A soil which is enriched with compost and used for a lawn, provides a dense mat of turf and enables the grass to withstand drought conditions. Ample

51

compost gives a "springy" type of lawn, of the best quality.

If one has an established, neglected lawn to deal with, the above dressing can be modified to equal parts of compost and sand to good effect.

DECEMBER.

There may be little to do in the flower garden this month, except to dig any empty beds, sort out staking material, tidy paths, and make plans for next season. There should be opportunity to attend to composting arrangements, making up a new bin, or preparing a fresh site for future compost making. Little compost making material may be available at this time, except perhaps for fallen leaves and household material. If any major alterations are planned, take advantage of frozen soil surface conditions to wheel soil or other material to fresh sites, this being more easily done under these conditions.

Chapter IV

Special Crops

1. Border Carnations.

2. Dahlias.

3. Early Flowering Chrysanthemums.

4. Roses.

5. Sweet Peas.

Border Carnations.

Border carnations, which are perennials, are often grown by themselves in a bed or border. They may also be included in the herbaceous border but are usually given pride of place in a situation by themselves.

They are especially sensitive to a badly drained site and frequently die off in winter because of this on a heavy soil. For this reason, it is best to grow them in a bed raised above the level of the surrounds, an arrangement which helps drainage considerably and cuts down winter losses.

Carnations are lime-loving plants and a generous amount of old mortar rubble (a 1in. layer is suitable), should be mixed in with the soil before they are planted. As well as this, give a 4oz. dressing of hydrated lime to each square yard. The raised plot or bed should be well dug by way of preparation and a 2in. layer of compost be lightly forked into the top 3ins. of soil just before planting. The bed should be trodden to firm it before planting commences.

It is possible to raise a batch of hardy border carnations from seed. Although only mixed colours may be obtained, and some "singles" which should be discarded, a fair percentage of large double flowers of good colours can be utilised for garden planting. Seed should be sown in a cold frame in

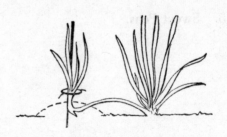

Fig. 7.—Layering border Carnations

spring, and seedlings transplanted out of doors in a sunny spot until planted in permanent positions in autumn. If one has plants already selected, new ones can be propagated by layering (see Fig. 7).

Briefly, suitable shoots are pegged down in the soil, a slit is cut in the stem at that point and the plant encouraged to make new roots from the exposed tissue.

The usual time for this method of propagation is July and August. The shoots growing on the outer part of the plant are most suitable. Remove the leaves from the part of the stem which will be in contact with the soil and cut into the stem as shown in the illustration. This slit is made by cutting through a leaf joint, and continuing the cut slanting lengthways up the stem.

Make a shallow hole where the layer will be, and mix coarse sand, compost and soil in equal parts, with which to cover the layered portion. The layered shoots must be kept in place with a wire peg.

A well established, selected plant may be large enough to have 6 or more layers taken from it. When rooted sufficiently, usually in 6 to 8 weeks, layers can be detached and planted in their permanent positions or left in position until the following spring, then lifted and replanted.

Propagation can also be done by cuttings. Use the tops of new, unflowered shoots, in June and July, and, leaving the tip intact, cut them 3ins. long and remove the lower two pairs of leaves. Trim the base neatly through a joint, with a sharp knife, and insert the cuttings firmly in pots of sand in a cold frame, or greenhouse. Keep the cuttings fairly "close", i.e., with little ventilation until they are rooted.

Plant most varieties 8 to 10ins. apart, but take special care with the depth of planting as this must be no deeper than the plants were previously—in pots or, if seedlings, in the border. During the growing season, disbud the flowering stems to leave one flower to each shoot and provide some thin stakes or supports to keep the stems upright. A ½in. mulch of compost in summer will encourage surface rooting and ensure moisture retention, as well as flowers of better quality.

One of the most serious troubles with border carnations is the disease called "Wilt". The affected plants turn yellow and the foliage dies off. Never use such plants for propagation purposes, either cuttings or layers. If diseased plants are present, always renew the soil mixture in the area they occupied.

Border carnations are often rather short-lived, and it is best to make provision for new plants, either by cuttings or layers, as a regular feature, thus ensuring a continuity of plants and flowers.

Varieties.—A selection of varieties, where plants are being purchased, can be made from :

Afterglow, yellow and red; Amy Robsart, white; Autocrat, red; Bookham Grand, crimson; Dainty, yellow and pink; Donns, apricot; Egret, white and pink; Ibis, carmine pink; Lilac Clove, Moonbeam, yellow; Red Ensign, scarlet; Southern Mist, heliotrope; Sprite, white and red; Vanessa, blush pink; Vivid, scarlet and Wild Rose, pink.

All reach 1½ to 2ft. high and are at their best in July.

Dahlias.

No late summer and autumn display is complete without some dahlias, and the taller varieties do best in a border by themselves. Even those of medium height—2½ft. or so—give a very good display if room allows for them to be given a separate position. In any case a row, or even a few plants of the medium decorative types, lend themselves very well to cutting purposes. (The dwarf bedding types have been described separately in Chapter 8.) A few dahlias may be planted in a mixed border, especially the taller ones, but the same general practices are adopted for these, as for a separate border. If one has plants already, the tubers should be lifted in autumn, when frost blackens the foliage. Leave about 6ins. of stem attached to them. There are many methods of storing dahlia tubers over winter but the basic requirements are cool, dry (not too dry), frost-proof conditions. Tubers are often kept in a shed, being protected in frosty spells with sacks or similar material. They should be dry when stored and if several named varieties are being grown, label each clump of tubers securely.

If one has a greenhouse and cuttings are wanted, plant the tubers to half their height in a box of suitable depth in February or March using peat or some soil and compost mixed, and start to water. When the new shoots are 3 to 4ins. long they can be detached and used for cuttings. Do not use very thick shoots as these do not root well. Trim the base neatly.

remove the lowest pair of leaves, then insert the cuttings firmly around the inside edge of a 5in. pot, in a compost of half sand and half peat, or vermiculite. When rooted move into 3½in. pots, singly, using a mixture of 3 parts loam, 2 parts compost and 1 part of coarse sand.

The plants will need hardening off prior to planting out of doors when danger of frost has passed, and the same general principles should be followed as given for hardening off bedding plants.

If no cuttings can be taken, the tuber clumps may be divided if large enough and planted out of doors in early May or later in cold areas. The young shoots may need some protection from late frosts. Old inverted 5in. pots are useful in this connection, or empty seed trays can be used in the early stages. Dahlias are particularly susceptible to frost damage and this point should be borne in mind.

Site.—The best position for dahlias is one in full sun, sheltered from cold winds, particularly from the north and east. Do not plant in shaded conditions or under the "drip" of trees.

Soil Preparation.—Dahlias are very gross feeders and for best results, dig in as much compost as can be spared. If a limited quantity only is available, add a 2in. layer of compost just prior to planting and fork this into the top few inches of soil. If both applications can be made, results will be better still.

Planting Distances.—If the very tall decorative varieties are being grown, these will need to be planted 3 to 4ft. apart.

The medium types need 2½ to 3ft. of space each way if tubers are being planted and slightly less if rooted cuttings are being used.

Planting.—If planting from pots, or putting in clumps of tubers, dig a hole large enough to take the ball of soil, or the tubers, without cramping. Plant the tubers so that the tops are covered by 2ins. of soil. Plant from pots so that the top of the ball of soil is slightly lower (½in.) than the general soil level.

After Planting.—Give each plant a cane or stake suitable to its height and tie securely, but avoid pulling the plant too tightly to the support. Further ties will be needed as growth is made (see Fig. 8).

Fig. 8.—Tying

Attention During Growth.—When the plants are about 15ins. high, top dress the soil around them with a 1in. layer of compost or, if this is not possible, use lawn mowings or spent hops. Try to cover a circle of 12ins. around the main stem.

The medium height varieties, if grown for decoration purposes only, will not need disbudding. If some of the buds are removed, however, the remaining flowers will be larger. Where the buds come in threes, remove the two side ones to obtain a single, large flower, or the centre one for two slightly smaller blooms.

Feeding.—If plants are given the generous basic treatment suggested, little further feeding will be needed, but if this is not possible give a further mulch of either compost, spent hops, or lawn mowings and water the plants with soot water, or liquid manure, once a week from the time they are 15ins. high, until the flower buds open. Use about ½-gallon to each plant at each application.

Varieties.—Some tall decorative, large-flowering varieties are :

58

Evelyn Ogg, violet, mauve; Frank Daws, crimson; Clara Cardew, pink; Searchlight, sulphur yellow; Diva, lilac; Mustang, rose pink; Edith Stokes, salmon; Betty Hone, mauve; Formality, orange and Jersey Beauty, salmon pink.

For a border devoted to the 3ft. varieties, use medium and small decorative types which are the most suitable for a small garden. Make your choice from the following, all of which can be relied upon for a good colour effect:

Newby, pink; Bloodstone, scarlet; Chorus Girl, pink; Edinburgh, maroon tipped white; Jescot Jim, yellow; Gerry Hoeck, pink; Jescot Purity, white; Jescot Hilda, purple, blue; Broadacre, orange; Lillian Bellegro, orange, apricot; Mary Broom, orange scarlet tipped white and Jescot Kenny, red tipped white.

Early Flowering Chrysanthemums.

This is the group of chrysanthemums which flower out of doors. By correct choice of varieties, a display can be obtained from August to the end of September. There is a risk of frost with the latest of the "early" varieties but for a bold splash of colour, the September flowering sorts are especially valuable.

To obtain the best results, devote a border to chrysanthemums alone. If only a limited space is available, a few plants can be incorporated into the herbaceous border, with good results. Most varieties are about 3ft. tall, so they will need to be sited amongst other plants of this height.

Choose a sunny border, yet a situation sheltered from wind. A well drained site is essential. Although dahlias make a large amount of surface roots, the plot should be forked or dug through before planting. Afterwards, add as generous a layer of compost as can be spared, forked into the top 6ins. of soil, where most of the roots will develop. Rake in a dressing of 4ozs. of bone meal and 4ozs. of wood ashes to each square yard, prior to planting. If the soil is new or not rich in compost, give 2ozs. of hoof and horn to each square yard as well.

Having dealt with the site preparation, we have now to go back to the taking of the cuttings, if stools are available, otherwise it means buying plants in for setting out in May.

Cuttings are best taken in a greenhouse, although they can be rooted in a cold frame in March. The new shoots that arise from the stools (last years plants) are used for propagation. Select those 3ins. long, remove the lower pair of leaves, leave the top intact, and cut through a leaf joint at the base, neatly with a sharp knife.

Small numbers of cuttings can be inserted in 5in. pots, about 2ins. apart, in a mixture of 2 parts loam, 1 part sieved compost and 1 part coarse grit. They can be rooted in pure sand, but this means moving them into pots as soon as they are rooted. There is always a danger of a check in growth, if repotting is delayed. Late February and early March is time enough to start taking cuttings in a greenhouse.

Firmly plant the prepared shoots to nearly half their depth and water them in. A high temperature is not needed: 50 degrees F. by night is ample. The cuttings will root more quickly if a sheet of polythene is laid over them, and this can rest lightly on the foliage. Examine the rooting medium for moisture content each day, but do not overwater, or some cuttings may be lost. The leaves may flag badly for 7 to 10 days, but this should not cause any concern, as they will recover. Rooting usually takes 3 to 4 weeks.

When this takes place, and the plants are "standing up" and new growth is being made, put the pots out in the open on a bench or staging in full light and continue to water with care.

The next job is to pot the plants singly into 3½in. pots. A good mixture to use is 3 parts loam, 2 parts sieved compost and 1 part coarse sand, with a handful each of bone meal, hoof and horn and wood ashes to each bucketful of the mixture. Place a little compost over the crocks in the bottom of the pot. The plants should be potted fairly firmly, and stood pot thick (that is, the pots touching) on the bench. Make sure that each variety is correctly labelled.

In late April, the plants can be stood out in a cold frame, but the pots should now be spaced out 1in. apart each way. Continue to water as needed, but only when the plants really need attention, as over watering must be avoided. At this stage each plant should have some support, with an 18in. thin, split cane. Do not tie too tightly: there should always be the space of two fingers between cane and plant. Hardening off the plants should follow the same lines as described for bedding plants in Chapter 7.

Planting should be done with care, each plant taken out of its pot with no disturbance to the roots. The crocks should be removed, and a hole taken out slightly larger than the ball of soil. The final planting depth should be such that the top of the ball is only slightly lower than the border level. The soil should be moderately firmed. Plants should be 15ins. apart each way, and a two or three row border will give a good display. After planting set a 4ft. cane in position to which the plants are tied, two or three times, as growth develops, the later tie encircling all the shoots.

When the plants are about 8 to 9 ins. high remove the growing point. This is called "stopping" and the aim is to make the plants "break", or send out side shoots. These are each allowed to bear one flower, at the top, and any side shoots that arise from the main breaks are removed when small. When the buds can be seen clearly at the ends of the shoots, remove all but the central bud. If all the buds are left, a "spray" of small flowers will be obtained, and there is no reason why a few plants should not be grown in this way.

Blooms of varying size can be obtained by reducing the number of main shoots (breaks) on each plant. If all are allowed to develop, the blooms may be small. For many varieties, 6 or 7 flowers per plant give good results, but if some plants are reduced to, say, 5 breaks, and others to 6, 7 or 8, flowers of contrasting size can be obtained.

When the plants are about 18ins. high, give a mulch, over the whole area if possible, of 1in. of compost, or if none can be spared, use lawn mowings, spent hops or leaf mould. Compost is to be preferred and some should be set aside for this purpose if at all possible.

During the growing season pay regular attention to tying, side shooting, disbudding, and the taking off of any shoots that arise from soil level or below.

Mention has been made in Chapter 9 of many of the pests that may attack chrysanthemums during the growing season. Regular spraying with Derris will keep the plants free of trouble in this respect.

61

There is one major point to remember concerning chrys-anthemum culture and that is to keep them growing without check, throughout, right from planting time. They respond to watering in dry spells, but with generous compost treatment will be well cared for in this respect, and will not suffer in dry weather, as much as do plants grown in soils poor in organic matter.

When flowering has finished, cut down the stems to 9ins., and lift the stools into a cold frame or into deep boxes. In either case, plant firmly and closely. Whether the stools are kept in a greenhouse or frame, protection from severe frost will be necessary. It is from these plants that cuttings can be taken, the following season. Keep the stools fairly dry over winter.

Varieties.—There are many scores of different sorts, if not hundreds, and to suggest but a few is very much a matter of personal choice. However, I have found from experience that the following can be relied on to give good results, and a colourful display, and if necessary are good for cutting also:

Appeal.—A free flowering red variety for August, and one that can confidently be included in the earlier flowering sorts.

Brenda Talbot.—The blooms have reflexed petals, that is they turn downwards, and are well shaped. The colour can best be described as carnation pink. It is September flowering and an attractive variety.

Chatsworth.—A very good orange bronze for August flowering, dwarf in habit, and good for spray or disbudded blooms of medium size.

Covent Garden.—A deep amber bloom, which makes an attractive display for September. It has very strong stems and is a variety the blooms of which stand up well to bad weather conditions.

Ermine.—An outstanding white variety, with incurving petals making a firm compact bloom. It is amongst the best of all in this colour. It is September flowering.

62

Florence Horwood.—A bright rose pink, with paler reverse. A good August variety, one of the best of this colour.

Harold Park.—A deep buttercup yellow, of medium vigour, for flowering in September and a "must" for a collection.

Peach Blossom.—A September flowering variety with silvery peach coloured blooms which make a bold display. One of the easiest of varieties to grow and one of the best for a border.

Red Flare.—This is an August flowering variety, the colour being a rich chestnut red. Not an over-vigorous variety but good for an early display.

A further selection can be made from, Alfreton Beauty, orange bronze (late August); Betty Riley, pink (August); Brumas, white (September); Derek Ellis, purple (September); Imperator, red (September); Migoli, yellow (September); Shirley Cream (September), and White Wings (September).

If one has neither greenhouse nor frame, plants will often overwinter out of doors in many districts but should be given protection with straw or bracken in cold areas. If plants do survive the winter, they should be divided in the spring, when new growth commences, and only the strongest rooted shoots kept. Replant on a fresh site and treat as for plants raised from cuttings, already described. Do not leave clumps unthinned or flowers will be small and results not as satisfactory as they should be.

Korean Chrysanthemums.—These are useful for September and October flowering, and even into November, if the weather is not too severe. They are of dwarf habit and need no staking. If a small border can be set aside for them, a colourful display of late flowers is assured. Some good varieties are: Apollo, bronze, single; Diane, pink, single; Mercury, salmon, single; Romany, crimson, double; and King Midas, yellow, double. These are amongst the latest subjects to flower under garden conditions.

Roses.

There are many who think that no garden is complete without roses. There is no need here to extol the virtues of these outstanding plants. There is certainly little to approach them for wealth of colour and diversity of interest. Although a whole book can be devoted to their cultivation, space precludes more than a survey of the main principles being dealt with here. It can be said however, that roses respond well to compost gardening and at least one bed should be set aside in a new garden for these attractive and colourful subjects.

Preparation for Planting.—As roses are to stay in the same place for many years, prepare for new plantings by digging the plot or bed to the full depth of the spade. Add as much compost as can be spared, at the same time, placing a generous layer in the bottom of each trench. Try to dig well beforehand so that the soil has time to settle, before planting. Good drainage is essential for roses and a shaded site should be avoided.

Manuring before Planting.—Rake in 3ozs. of Bone Meal and 4ozs. dry wood ash, to each square yard, a week or so prior to planting. If enough compost is available, lightly fork in a 2in. layer, just before planting is done, but make sure that this is kept in the top few inches of soil. Firm the soil by treading if it is at all loose.

Planting.—Bushes should be planted as soon as they are received in autumn, so long as the soil is not too wet. If it is, plant the bushes temporarily (called heeling in) until conditions improve. When the soil is dry enough, dig out a hole large enough to take the roots without cramping and to such a depth that the planted bush will be the same depth as before. The soil mark, showing previous planting depth, will be seen on the stem.

It is important not to plant too deeply, for if the point at which the bud was inserted (the union) is buried the rose itself will root. The effect of the root portion (the root stock) is then lost.

Delphiniums. No herbaceous border should be without some of these majestic subjects

Plant firmly, treading the soil as necessary, and place a 2in. mulch of compost all round the bushes after planting. Make sure that each bush or each bed is labelled correctly.

Planting Distances.—The dwarf varieties should be given 18 to 20 ins. apart each way, and the stronger growing varieties 21 to 24ins. If in doubt, check from a rose catalogue whether or not the variety concerned is a strong growing sort.

If an old rose bed has to be dealt with, in which there are many blank spaces, rather than plant new bushes in these gaps it is a better plan to make an entirely new bed or beds. Some of the existing bushes in the old bed can be moved, so that they form a complete display in themselves. If this is impossible and new bushes have to be planted in the old bed, take out 15ins. of the existing soil and replace with a mixture of new soil well enriched with compost, equal parts of each if possible. This should be done for each new planting site, not the whole bed.

Pruning.—Newly-planted bush roses should be cut back to about two or three buds after planting. The tops of the cuts should be slightly slanting, and just above the uppermost bud.

Established bush roses can be pruned in the same way, cutting back the growth made that year to two or three buds. Very strong growing varieties like Peace can be pruned more lightly. Any dead wood, or very weak shoots should be cut out altogether. The time of pruning is usually late March but many bushes are now pruned in early winter.

During the summer, on newly planted and established roses, make full use of any spare lawn mowings as a mulch for the rose bed. Do not apply a thick layer at any one time; a 1in. dressing is ample. Such a mulch will keep down much of the weed growth but any that does appear can be dug out, or pulled up by hand and used in the compost heap. The mulch, plus the compost used in spring, will do much towards building up a reserve of soil moisture for use in dry spells, which is an important point with roses.

In summer cut back the spent blooms as soon as they go over, to just above a growth bud. This should be done regu-

65

larly and all such material cut off can be put on the compost heap.

The main job to do in autumn is to fork through the beds lightly, thus burying any mulching material that remains. All fallen foliage should be raked up first and composted in the centre of a well-made heap. Be careful not to fork too deeply, close up to the bushes themselves.

Some Good Varieties of Hybrid Teas and Hybrid Perpetuals.—There is such a range of varieties, in such diversity of colours, that the choice, for a beginner, or indeed an experienced gardener, can be bewildering. One's own fancy should be followed, based on varieties seen at public parks, shows, at nurseries or in other gardens. Usually if a bed of 6, 12 or more new bushes is being planned for, a fairly wide range of colours is preferred. To help in such a choice, any of the following varieties can be chosen with confidence.

Crimson Glory.—A very deep crimson rose with a dark velvet sheen, still amongst the most popular. It is very free flowering, of upright habit and well scented.

Eden Rose.—This is a coral pink with a silver sheen, and bears large blooms. It has fairly strong growth and is highly scented.

Josephine Bruce.—A bright deep red, large blooms and low growing habit. The flowers are long lasting and scented.

Peace.—A very vigorous variety, which should be planted with other strong-growing sorts. It has large well shaped blooms, yellow in bud, edged with pink, later becoming yellow, cream and pink. One bush at least is a "must", and can be planted in the centre of the bed if other weaker growing sorts are included with it.

Speks Yellow.—A good variety with bold shining yellow blooms of medium size borne in clusters on upright stems. A nicely scented variety and one of the best yellows.

66

Sultane.—A brilliant vermilion scarlet with an orange flush and a golden yellow reverse. The flowers are freely borne; the growth is slender. A very colourful variety for a small bed.

Violinista Costa.—This is a good garden variety, coral orange and pink in colour. The flowers are of medium size and the growth compact in habit.

Virgo.—One of the best white varieties, with stronger than average growth. It has well shaped buds, and in a mixed bed provides a good contrast in colour. It is of upright habit and scented.

A further choice can be made from: McGredys Ivory, creamy white; Monique, pink; Karl Herbst, red; Lydia, yellow; Mrs. G. A. van Rossen, golden orange; Ena Harkness, red, and Tzigane, orange pink.

Hybrid Polyantha or Floribunda Roses.

These are roses which bear large trusses, or clusters of flowers, most of which may open at the same time, and which are very popular for bedding purposes. Here again the choice of varieties is very wide but any of the following can be chosen with confidence.

Fashion.—Flowers are salmon pink, and the buds particularly well shaped. The growth is of medium vigour and flowers are borne over a long period.

Frensham.—This is a deep crimson with semi-double flowers borne in large, bold clusters. It is an outstanding variety and deservedly very popular.

Goldilocks.—As the name implies, this rose is a rich golden yellow. The flowers are double and borne in bold clusters. Growth is dwarf in habit, and the flowering season longer than with many varieties.

Independence.—A fairly vigorous variety with large flowers, vermilion in colour and freely borne. It is best to remove the old flowers regularly as they fade.

Masquerade.—Of fairly vigorous growth, with flowers borne in large clusters, orange then crimson as they open. An unique variety for colouring but one of the easiest to grow.

Polly Prim.—A good variety of medium vigour and bushy habit. The large, lemon yellow flowers are borne in bold sprays, making an eye catching display.

A further choice can be made from: Concerto, orange scarlet; Korona, scarlet; Moulin Rouge, crimson scarlet; Orange Triumph, orange crimson; Spartan, salmon orange; Sundance, yellow pink, and Ingrid Stenzig, pink.

Rambler Roses.

Rambler roses are without equal for covering a pergola or fence, for growing against a wall that needs covering to take away the "bare" effect, and for providing at the same time a wealth of colour in the summer months. In many gardens only two or three varieties may need to be considered. These may well be chosen from the most popular, well-tried sorts, and any of the varieties described below can be purchased with confidence.

Alberic Barbier, white; Albertine, copper pink; Crimson Conquest, red; Chaplins Pink; Dr. Van Fleet, pink; Climbing Orange Triumph; Sanders White and Francois Juranville, pink.

Pruning Rambler Roses.—The shoots which have borne the flowers are cut out, down to soil level, in autumn. New shoots, that is those which have made their growth the same season, are kept and tied in securely to the pillar, pergola or fence. These shoots are not shortened. It is these that will give the flower display next year. Should there be but a few shoots (new), one or two of the old growths can be kept, but all the side shoots on these should be cut back to two buds.

With rambler roses, the best way to plant cuttings, which can be inserted out of doors, is to prepare the soil in the border (not too sunny, and sheltered), making it very loose and friable, and mixing silver sand and leaf compost or peat with it, so that it is moderately dry. Press the cuttings, which should be 10ins. long, firmly (this is most important) around the stem of each. The cuttings may be planted quite close together, i.e. 6ins. or so apart, and are best taken in early autumn.

Climbing Roses.

These do well on the walls of a house, except the north aspect, or for growing against a fence or on pillars. A few very popular varieties are:

Gloire de Dijon, a creamy yellow, which is one of the few varieties which succeed on a north wall. Climbing Speks yellow; Madame Alfred Carriere, white; which will do fairly well in a sunless position. Climbing Crimson Glory, red; Pauls Scarlet, the well known rosy scarlet variety seen in many gardens. Madame G. Staechelin, rosy pink, and Climbing Caroline Testout, silvery pink.

Pruning Climbing Roses.—Varieties such as Pauls Scarlet, Alberic Barbier and Chaplins Pink, are pruned in a similar manner, except that there may be fewer new shoots from ground level, to deal with. In this case, shorten some of the old shoots back to within 18ins. of ground level, to encourage a supply of new growth. The existing new shoots are retained, full length, and older growths either cut out or shortened back to where a new shoot can take its place.

With other varieties, in general, leave in as much young growth as is possible, so long as the space available is not overcrowded. Old shoots can be cut out, if thin and weak, and any lateral growths remaining on old wood shortened back to two buds. Any dead pieces of wood should be cut out.

Sweet Peas.

These, one of the most popular annuals, grown for both cutting and decoration, are best given a position by themselves. Sweet peas are usually grown in a well prepared trench which can be taken out in readiness during winter. It is best to grow two rows of plants to the trench if each plant is to be staked separately (this is the best method if quality blooms are required), so the trench will need to be 15 to 18ins. wide. Dig out the soil to the depth of the spade and fork up the base to the full depth of the fork. Next, place a 4 to 6in. layer of compost on top of this forked soil and mix it in with the loose soil. Fill in half the remaining space in the trench with the soil dug out, place a further layer of compost on this and, again, fork this in as well. The finished level will be higher than the surrounding soil but will sink slightly over winter. A shallow depression will be needed for planting so some soil may need to be removed.

Prior to planting in early April, scatter 4ozs. of bone meal and 4ozs. of wood ash, over the trench area, and rake this in so that it is mixed with the top 4 or 5ins. of trench. When this is done sprinkle hydrated lime over the planting area at 2ozs. to each square yard. To get early flowers of extra good quality sow seeds in 3in. pots in cold frames in October. Guard against mice, which may eat the seeds readily. Give as much ventilation as possible after germination, and water only moderately. A good seed-sowing compost is 3 parts loam, 1 part sieved compost and 1 part coarse sand. Make sure the pots are well "crocked", as good drainage is important for sweet peas both in the propagation stages and later.

Stop the plants, that is take the growing point out, when they are about 5ins. high. This encourages strong "breaks" or side shoots which, later, should be reduced to leave the best one.

If the plants are to be supported by pea sticks, i.e. not tied into canes and grown on a single stem, the number of growths (shoots) per plant can be two or three. More flowers will be obtained this way but they will be of smaller size.

For planting from pots, knock out the plant and ball of soil by tapping the inverted pot on something solid (supporting the plant between the fingers), and remove the crocks. Make a hole with the trowel slightly larger than the ball of soil but of the same depth or only very slightly deeper. Set the ball of soil in position, firm the surrounding soil to it, and water in. If planting two rows in the trench, these should be 8ins. apart. The plants can be 6ins. apart. Plant firmly and water in. Support the plants with short twiggy growths in the early stages if canes are not used. This will also give some protection from cold winds. To get the very best results, tie the plants to 6, 7 or 8ft canes and secure them to these supports regularly with fillis string, raffia, wire rings or twist ties, all of which can be bought in most garden sundries shops.

If one has no canes, strings can be used but these will need to be stretched tightly to a wire 6ft. from ground level. This means that stout posts will be needed at each end of the row to take the wire. Posts and wire will be needed if canes are employed as supports.

If pea sticks are used, hazel wood is best but any well-branched "twiggy" material, 6ft. high if possible, can be utilised. Set the sticks firmly in position, sharpening the ends first if they are rather thick.

Where the plants are tied to canes, tie them in regularly, remove the tendrils and take out the side shoots when small. Any shoots that arise from the base of the main stem, should also be removed when small.

During the early stages of growth, sweet peas will benefit from a mulch of lawn mowings, especially during May and June if the weather is warm, a 1in. layer being sufficient to help conserve moisture. Water the plants once a week with liquid manure for best quality flowers and, if very hot spells occur, give a good soaking with clear water if the plants flag.

During the evening of hot days, damp the foliage with clean water, using a rosed can or a hose with the end pinched between thumb and finger. This will be of great benefit and will also help to prevent bud drop.

Varieties.—There are very many sweet pea varieties and it is difficult to reduce them to, say 12 outstanding sorts. The following can, however, be relied upon to give pleasure and a wide variety of colour.

Air Warden, orange, cerise; Cream Gigantic; Princess Elizabeth, salmon; Christina, rose; Elizabeth Taylor, mauve; Carlotta, carmine; Mrs. R. Bolton, rose pink; Red Velvet, deep crimson; Valerie, white; Stylish, blue; Classic, purple, and Gertrude Tingay, lavender.

Chapter V

Bulbs and Corms

1. Grown out of doors.

2. Grown in pots or bowls.

General Points

There is a wide range of bulbs and corms that may be grown out of doors, some in beds for spring flowering (such as daffodils, narcissi and tulips), some as edging plants (like crocus), and some in groups in mixed or other borders (like gladioli). Of the many types available, the following are amongst the most popular and the most easily grown. Where applicable, some suitable and easily grown varieties are given in each case.

Daffodils in Beds.

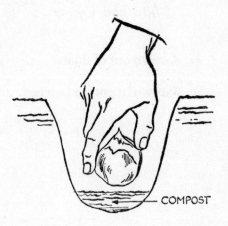

Fig. 9.—When planting bulbs singly, a hole amply large enough for the bulbs should be lined with sand if the soil is heavy

Bulbs should be planted in September and can be spaced 6ins. apart and 4ins. deep (see Fig. 9). Well dug soil is needed, and a 2in. dressing of compost should be forked into the top 4ins. of soil prior to planting. An application of wood ashes at 4ozs. to the square yard will also be of benefit.

For details of varieties, please see the section headed "Bulbs in Pots and Bowls", later in this chapter.

Tulips.

For outdoor planting in beds, tulips should be planted 6ins. apart and 4ins. deep. The main period of planting is September and October. Tulips do well in most soils, except the very heavy type, and if this is being dealt with, add a handful of coarse sand, to the bottom of the planting hole. Try to avoid planting in the same piece of ground or in the same bed two years running. Tulips do best in soil that has not been occupied by tulips for some time.

When planning to have more than one type of these colourful subjects, remember that the early single tulips are the first to flower, followed by the early double types. Mendel and Triumph tulips flower in April, whilst for May a choice can be made from the Darwin, Cottage or Breeder types, which flower in that order.

Early Double Tulips.—These are not perhaps as popular as other types, but nevertheless make a good contrast. Popular varieties are: Dante, blood red; Murillo Max, rose flushed white; Orange Nassau, orange scarlet and Peach Blossom, rosy pink.

Breeder Tulips.—These are slightly taller than the Darwins and have large flowers in a wide colour range. A few popular sorts are, Dillenburg, salmon orange; Pontiac, mahogany red and President Hoover, tangerine scarlet.

Cottage Tulips.—Some good varieties are: Belle Jaune, yellow; Advance, orange scarlet; Carrara, white; Mrs. John T. Scheepers, yellow; Rosy Wings, salmon pink and Renown, carmine red.

Early Single Tulips.—These are not so large as the May flowering tulips but are useful if an early batch is required. They are mostly 12 to 15ins. tall. A few good varieties are: Brilliant Star, scarlet; Ibis, rose pink; Mon Tresor, yellow; Prince of Austria, orange scarlet, and Princess Irene, salmon orange.

Mendel Tulips.—These flower 10 days earlier than the Darwins, and follow the Early Singles. Krelage Triumph, geranium red, is a popular variety, and Orange Wonder is also good. Emmy Peck, lilac rose, can also be recommended.

Triumph Tulips.—These follow on after the Mendel types, and some good varieties are, Elmus, cherry red edged with white; Johanna, salmon pink; Paris, orange red edged yellow and Red Giant.

Darwin Tulips.—These, widely used for beds, are available in a very wide colour range. All are about 24 to 30ins. high. A few very popular varieties are: Bartigon, cochineal red; Charles Needham, red; Farncombe Sanders, geranium red; Golden Harvest, yellow; Queen of the Bartigons, salmon pink; Prunus, rose pink; and Hollands Glory, scarlet. It is also possible to buy a mixture of colours, which will ensure a widely contrasting range of shades for bedding purposes. However, it is usually best to plant one variety to one bed if a definite colour scheme is wanted.

Hyacinths.

Outside planting can be done from September to November. Hyacinths do best in a light new soil, to which ample organic manure has been added. Drainage must be good. Do not plant when the soil is very wet. Set the bulbs in holes made with a trowel, 5ins. deep.

Some protection may be needed from straw or leaf mould, in very hard weather. Some varieties that are suitable for outdoor planting are: King of the Blues, a deep indigo blue; Grand Maitre, lavender blue; Queen of the Pinks, and Jan Bos, red.

Smaller bulbs can be used for outdoor planting than for culture in pots and bowls.

Chinodoxa.

Often called Glory of the Snow, these bulbs give a brilliant display in March and April. Plant in Autumn, setting the bulbs 3ins. deep. They are fully hardy and may be used for naturalizing.

Several shades of blue are available, and there is also a pink variety. A blue like that of C. Sardensis is usually most popular.

Crocus.

Being one of the first flowers in the spring, crocus are especially valuable and, with the wide range of colour, are particularly pleasing. The bulbs should be planted 2 or 3ins. apart in bold groups in autumn, in holes 3ins. deep. They can be left undisturbed for some years. Crocus can be grown in bowls but must be given cool conditions or they may not flower. The large Dutch varieties are very good for a spring display. A few varieties from the wide choice available are: Excelsior, lilac blue; Queen of the Blues, Remembrance, purple; Snowstorm, white and Mammoth, yellow.

Cyclamen (Hardy).

These miniature species are useful plants for a shaded position and will do well beneath trees. They need a well-drained position and some lime rubble should be mixed in with the soil.

They are all of dwarf habit and should be planted as soon as they are received. It is sometimes necessary to order the bulbs in advance and this should be done in July. The varieties include C. Neapolitunum, which is autumn flowering and has rose pink flowers; C. Coum Roseum, flowering in February or March, pink in colour, and C. Vernum, which has crimson flowers, borne in April and May.

Gladioli.

These are very valuable plants for a separate border or for using in a mixed border. They may also be planted in gaps in a herbaceous border. Corms are set, in April, in holes 3ins. deep and 6 to 8ins. apart. At the end of the season, lift the corms, and store them in a dry cool place. Take off the remains of the stem and any loose outer scales, then store the corms in a shallow tray. The choice of varieties is very wide, but the following are of high quality : Abu Hassan, violet; Hopmans Glory, yellow, and Lavender Dream, all early. Bit of Heaven, orange; General Eisenhower, salmon pink; Mrs. Marks Memory, carmine, and Picardy, pink, for mid season flowering. New Europe, salmon orange, and Spotlight, yellow and scarlet, for later flowering.

Scillias.

These "bluebells" are useful for shaded positions where many other plants will not succeed. Plant 4ins. deep in September. They flower in May and June and are very colourful. The variety Blue Queen is very striking; Blue Giant is also a good sort, while Myosotis is a lighter blue.

Snowdrops.

As one of the first flowers in late winter, room should be found for at least a few snowdrops, and these can be naturalized in a partly shaded position. Set the bulbs nearly touching and 2ins. deep. The common snowdrop, Galanthus Nivalis, has single flowers and is the well known variety, but the variety Corcyrensis should also be planted. This has a long season of flowering, but bulbs should be planted as soon as possible, in September. An order should be placed in July.

Bulbs in Pots and Bowls.

Daffodils and Narcissi.

These may be grown in a mixture of 2 parts leaf mould (or peat), 1 part soil and 1 part coarse sand, or in bulb fibre and a little charcoal and silver sand, the latter being obtainable from garden sundries shops. Varieties to flower at Christmas, like Soleil d'Or and Paper White, should be planted not later than early September; if these are available in August, so much the better.

The main batch of varieties such as Rembrandt and Golden

Harvest (both good large trumpet varieties), Fortune, Geranium and Carlton, should be planted in October for March flowering. It is a good policy to plant at intervals, thus ensuring a long display of flowers.

If the bulbs for indoor flowering are in pots, with drainage holes, provision must be made for drainage. Arrange a layer of "crocks" (broken pots), about an inch deep at the bottom of the pot. Nearly fill the pots with fibre or bulb compost (use the latter for bowls), firm it slightly and plant the bulbs nearly touching, at such a depth that the tops only protrude above the fibre. Leave sufficient room for watering—about ½in. in a 5in. pot.

A 5in. pot is convenient for most daffodils and narcissi, and will take 3 double-nosed bulbs (see Fig. 10) of average size. Set the bulbs firmly and firm the fibre or bulb compost with the fingers.

Fig. 10.—Double-nosed Narcissus bulb

The planting medium should be moist for best results. Keep the pots or bowls in a cupboard, or similar dark place, until the green tips of the leaves appear above the soil. They can also be plunged out of doors and covered with a 4in. layer of soil or fine ashes.

If the pots or bowls are kept in the dark, bring them out into the light when the shoots are 3ins. high. Stand them on a sunny window sill and examine daily for water requirement.

If plunged out of doors, bring the bulbs inside when the leaves are about 3ins. high. This will mean examining them after about 6 to 8 weeks in the "plunge".

The taller varieties will need some small stakes, as support, and thin material, like raffia, used for tying. The cooler one can grow daffodils and narcissi the sturdier the growth, and the longer the flowers will last, although the flowering period will be delayed slightly. As the leaves grow more freely, more water will be needed. Move the pots or bowls slightly each day, to obtain balanced growth.

Bulbs that have been grown in fairly cool conditions can be planted out of doors the following August. Continue to give water after the flowers go over, until the foliage dies down naturally.

Hyacinths in Pots or Bowls.

Bulbs should be planted in September for Christmas flowering and specially prepared bulbs, which will flower earlier than un-prepared, can be obtained. These should be planted as soon as purchased.

Later planting will mean later flowering; i.e. October planting gives flowers in March, under "home" conditions (i.e. not forced).

Hyacinths can be planted 3 bulbs to a bowl, and should be 1in. apart. The depth of planting is such that the nose or tip of the bulb just protrudes above soil level. Plant firmly.

Hyacinths can be kept in a dark place indoors or plunged out of doors as are daffodils. After about 3 months, bring the bowls into warmth, but keep fairly cool until the flower bud is clear of the neck of the bulb.

A neat stake and tie, may be needed for each hyacinth but, here again, grow under as cool conditions as possible, for long-lasting flowers.

Hyacinth Varieties.

Bismark.—This is a very good light blue variety, and does well for early flowering in pots and bowls.

King of the Blues.—This is a late variety and is an attractive indigo blue, having a very large spike.

Jan Bos.—A good variety for growing indoors. The flowers are red and keep their colour well.

L'Innocence.—For a white variety this is often the first choice. It is good for pots, bowls or bedding purposes.

Pink Pearl.—This, a clear pink, is a favourite for indoor growing. The spike is broad and makes a bold display.

Myosotis.—A light blue variety with large bells, forming a good spike. It is a very good variety for growing in bowls.

Lady Derby.—Grown for bedding and in pots. It is a salmon pink and makes a good display.

Daffodil and Narcissi Varieties.

Trumpet Narcissi.
Golden Harvest.—This is one of the largest-flowered varieties, rather tall for growing in bowls but a very easy variety to grow. It is one of the earliest to flower and a "must" for outdoor planting.

Rembrandt.—This is another very good variety, especially suitable for pots and bowls due to its moderate height. It is another early-flowering variety. Its flowers are large and golden yellow in colour.

Queen of Bicolours.—This variety has a white perianth and canary yellow trumpet. It is a strong grower and one of the best garden varieties.

Large Cupped Narcissi.
Aranjuez.—This is a good variety for growing in pots or out of doors. It is a vigorous grower and the flowers are especially attractive. The perianth is yellow and the cup (trumpet) margined with orange red.

O F G—6

Fortune.—This is one of the best varieties in this group. Although rather tall, it does very well in pots or bowls as well as out of doors. It has a lemon yellow perianth, and a copper-orange cup.

Semper Avanti.—This does well both out of doors and in pots or bowls. It has a creamy white perianth, and an orange cup.

Small Cupped Narcissi.
La Riante.—Like the rest of this group, this variety has smaller flowers than the varieties already mentioned. The white, flat perianth and crimson scarlet cup make this a most attractive variety for pots, bowls or outside.

Double Narcissi.
These are not generally so popular as the other types, but the double trumpet daffodil, Van Sion, is grown both in pots and outside. It is good for early flowering in pots and also for naturalizing out of doors.

Triandus Narcissi.
These are sometimes grown on the rock garden, and are also very suitable for growing in pots or bowls. One attractive variety is Shot Silk, which has several small flowers on a stem, all creamy white. It grows 12 to 15ins. high and for a bowl of bulbs with a difference can be thoroughly recommended.

Cyclamineus Narcissi.
These too, are useful for rock garden plantings, or in pots and bowls. An especially useful, easy to grow variety is March Sunshine. It is one of the earliest to flower in March, with reflexed yellow petalled flowers. It is very free flowering, and would be my choice if only one variety could be grown.

Jonquils.
These have a charm of their own and the variety Campernelli, Orange Queen, is scented, with 3 or 4 golden orange flowers to each stem. It does well in pots and bowls.

Tazetta Narcissi.

These varieties have several flowers to a stem, and one of the easiest to grow is Geranium. It has broad, white petals with an orange scarlet cup. It does very well out of doors and also in pots.

Poeticus Narcissi.

The best known variety in this group is Actea—the Pheasant Eye type, and the broad flat, white flowers with the dark red eye, are particularly attractive.

The Miniature Narcissi.

These make very good plants for pots and bowls, especially the varieties 5 or 6ins. in height. They do best if grown as cool as possible, and should not be forced. If the bulbs are very small, some sorts may not flower during the first year. Plant the bulbs about 1in. apart in bowls rather than pots. Some suitable species are H. Bulbocodium Conspicuus; N. Canaliculatus and N. Minimus, which is only 3ins. high. All these can be grown on the rockery as well as in bowls. If in the latter, stand them outside after flowering and keep well watered until the foliage dies down naturally.

Naturalised Bulbs.

This means bulbs that are planted out of doors, often in grass, in fairly large groups. If the soil is very heavy use the stronger-growing varieties like the trumpet and large cupped sorts. Depth of planting should be 4 or 5ins. and this should be done in September and October.

Chapter VI

Plants in and Around the Home.

1. Pot Plants in the Home.

    Management, General Points.

    Christmas Pot Plants.

    Pot Plant Problems.

    Some Fuchsia Pointers.

    Miniature Roses as Pot Plants.

    Impatiens.

    Watering.

    Feeding.

    House Plants.

2. Hanging Baskets.

3. Window Boxes.

Pot Plants in the Home.

Management, General Points.—Assuming that one does not have a greenhouse, and any pot plants have to be purchased, the following general points should be borne in mind. An even temperature is essential as nothing will cause poor results with pot plants more quickly than very warm evening conditions and cold night temperatures. Hot, stuffy rooms are also very detrimental. A cool room is best, a cool windowsill being very suitable. Avoid standing plants in draughts as these will check growth very quickly, and can cause the death of many subjects.

Try to give pot plants in the home good light conditions. This may not always be possible, but bear this point in mind, as it is important. Always keep pot plants away from fires, or the heat of lights.

Christmas Pot Plants.—Where pot plants new to one have been received as Christmas gifts, the following are some of the points which may arise regarding their management.

Should the pot plant be un-named, and its name not yet known, watering may be the main problem. In general, water only moderately, keeping the compost just damp and, usually, if in any doubt, delay watering for the time being.

Where one has received leafy subjects like Sansevieria, Ficus or Hedera (ivy), these will definitely benefit from having the foliage sponged over with a soft cloth and some tepid soapy water from time to time. No plant will do well if there is a coating of dust on its foliage. This sponging will also improve the appearance of the plants considerably.

If one has been fortunate enough to have been given an Azalea, the flowering life of this colourful subject can be considerably prolonged by picking off the dead flowers regularly, and above all, by not over-watering. If this is done, i.e. too much water given, the foliage will start to fall. The cooler this plant can be kept, and evenly cool at that, the longer it will stay in flower. It is worth persevering with to get the best from it, as with care it will give further pleasure in succeeding years.

The popular berried plant—the Solanum, often called the

"winter cherry", is frequently purchased for the Christmas period, or may be received as a present. It does quite well under home conditions, but care should be taken with the watering, for too much moisture causes the leaves to drop. The plants and berries can be kept in good condition for the longest time in an evenly cool, draught-free room. The whole plant can be washed under a tap, to clean off any dust that may collect on leaves or berries.

Solanums can be kept from year to year, but are best raised from seed sown under glass in February or of course, fresh plants may be purchased each December.

With hyacinths which are in full bloom over Christmas the longest pleasure can be obtained by cutting off the fading flowers, i.e. the individual "florets", at the base of the spike as they "go over". When all the flowers are over, continue to water the plant as usual; do not allow the foliage to shrivel for lack of moisture, and stand the pot in cool conditions indoors for the time being. The bulbs can later be planted out of doors or given to someone who can plant them outside. Cut off the whole of the "spike" when flowering is over.

Cyclamen often take pride of place regarding a Christmas present. To prolong flowering, pick off any dead blooms as they fade. If this is done regularly, the life of the plant will be much lengthened. Any dead or yellow leaves at the base of the plant can also be picked off.

St. Paulia (the African Violet), one of the likely Christmas gifts, will need the most careful attention. It needs a higher temperature and a more moist atmosphere than the other subjects mentioned. When watering this plant keep the water off the foliage for cold water can cause yellow markings which detract from the appearance of the plant.

Remember that no plant likes being in a draught and often a window-sill may not be the best position especially in colder weather. A draught-free, even temperature is best for the long lasting of flowering pot plants. Disappointing results will be obtained if plants are kept in very warm rooms.

Pot Plant Problems.—"Why do the leaves drop ...?" One of the most common problems met with in pot plants under home conditions, is that of the "leaves falling off". This happens with a wide range of subjects, not only to those which are normally used to a warmer atmosphere.

Over-watering is a frequent cause of leaf drop, probably one of the most common causes, but normally the trouble is past repair when it is realised that too much water is at fault. At the first signs of leaf drop make sure that too much water is not given subsequently.

Where plants are purchased, see that they are well protected in the journey between nursery or shop and the home. Keep them out of draughts and well wrapped up, especially in windy or frosty weather. Keep all pot plants out of draughts when indoors. This is often the cause of the foliage being shed or of the plants looking unhappy.

Keep all pot plants in as even a temperature as possible; there is nothing worse than excess warmth by day and cold at night. An evenly cool room or window-sill is better than too high a temperature. Err towards cooler rather than warmer conditions if doubt exists, except where it is known that the pot plants concerned are definitely better in fairly high temperatures.

Some Fuchsia Pointers.—As a pot plant in the home, fuchsias are very popular for a summer display, but one frequently hears complaints that "the flowers drop off". In many cases this is due to keeping the plants in too confined an atmosphere, i.e. not giving them enough ventilation. They appreciate a position in well ventilated rooms and will certainly not do well in warm conditions.

Some fuchsia flowers fall off with age in any case but this is different from all the blooms falling off at one time. Over-watering and under-watering should be guarded against, either of which will cause the blooms to drop.

If a fuchsia plant is being purchased as a gift or for ones own pleasure there is a wealth of varieties available. I have found the following to be the most popular: Ballet Girl; Fascination and Prince Charming. Any one of these varieties can be relied upon to give pleasure.

Miniature Roses as Pot Plants.—It is always an extra pleasure to have a present with a difference. A miniature rose

88

as a pot plant gift, either if one is the giver or the receiver, can be relied upon in this connection.

It should be borne in mind, however, that these plants with their fine root system need rather careful watering. In my experience, over-watering is the chief cause of trouble.

I find that a not too rich compost is best, and little feeding, so that the plants remain fairly compact in habit. Misplaced and unbalanced growths should be cut back with small nail scissors as necessary.

Wash the foliage from time to time, with a small sponge, to avoid dust collecting. Some varieties which I find suitable include Baby Gold, this being one of the larger miniature sorts, and best, I think, in the bud stage. A very fine flowering pink is Cinderella, which is another I prefer when it is in bud. Pour Toi, is a charming, creamy white variety, especially suitable as a "special" gift, and Tom Thumb an attractive red.

Impatiens.—Busy Lizzie, as it is called, is a very popular pot plant for home conditions. The variety I. Sultanii, is frequently met with and its scarlet flowers are borne freely.

Plants should be cut back in March to encourage fresh growth for the summer. Less water should be given in winter. Cuttings will root very readily and new growths 2ins. long can be inserted in sand, or even in a glass of water, where they provide interest in forming roots quickly. If this method is used, the plants should be potted up as soon as roots form freely.

Details of several other pot plants that can be grown under "home" conditions are given in Chapter 7 (Greenhouse and Conservatory Plants).

Watering.—The same general principles apply as have been stressed in Chapter 7 on watering pot plants in the greenhouse or conservatory. Make sure that the pots stand in a suitable saucer or shallow pan to collect water that drains through. Plants can, of course, be watered in the kitchen sink and allowed to "drain" before being put back in their original position.

Where practicable, always stand plants out in the rain, in spring and summer, so that as well as the watering aspect, the foliage benefits from the effect of moisture—always an important point with plants grown indoors.

Where the lady of the house has to see to the watering of pot plants, the Christmas period presents some new problems. If one has bulbs in bowls to deal with, and these have no drainage holes, make sure that too much water is not given. Tip these bowls on their sides, carefully, after watering, so that any surplus can drain off. Bulbs, whether daffodils, hyacinths or tulips, will not stand water lying at their roots.

With bulbs in bowls, the best way to check the fibre or compost for actual water requirement, is to "feel" it with the fingers. If in doubt, delay watering for the time being. Bowls can also be tapped with a knife handle, or something similar, to see if they "ring", which they will, if dry. If there is only a dull thud on such tapping being done, do not water. Where several plants are to be checked for watering, it is surprising how, with a little practice, one can detect the differences in tone one gets on tapping, according to the varying stages of dryness or wetness of the compost.

When a pot is dry, fill up the available space with water more than once, if needs be. Allow the first applications to drain through, before giving more. When the compost is really wet, no more water will be needed perhaps for some days.

If the water does not drain through a pot as quickly as it should, make sure that the crocking is adequate. If in doubt, take the plant out of its pot, by turning it upside down, and tapping the rim on the edge of a table, keeping the fingers of one hand across the ball of soil and also around the plant's stem, to prevent it falling. If more crocking appears to be necessary, remove the existing pieces, and put fresh ones in the bottom of the pot.

Feeding Pot Plants.—Under home conditions, the easiest method of feeding pot plants is to use one of the proprietary liquid organic "feeds". There are several very good preparations which I have used with the greatest satisfaction. Whichever is used, follow the maker's instructions closely regarding mixing with water and the frequency of application.

House Plants.—Of recent years, these have become very

popular, most of them being foliage plants. Some are climbing subjects and, in general, the same principles of management apply as for flowering pot plants.

An extra factor however, is the removal of dust from the leaves, of the larger-leaved subjects especially of which the India Rubber Plant (Ficus) is a good example. This, and other foliage plants, will benefit considerably by having the leaves sponged once a week with tepid soapy water. They will derive benefit from this in other ways, as well as being made more attractive in appearance.

With house plants in mind, as a special treat for one's self buy three plants in 3in. pots, and set them in a suitable bowl for a small table, or windowsill, where they can be seen by visitors. A suitable choice of plants which I know will give pleasure, is Peperomia Glabella, with its neat variegated foliage, of compact habit, and Tradescantia Golden Queen, and also Silver Queen. This blend gives contrast and attractiveness.

Regarding the bowl in which to plant them, a suitable type can be purchased from most gardens sundries shops. One 6ins. in diameter, will be suitable and, if of a fawn colour, will give a pleasing contrast to the plants mentioned above.

Other possibilities which may be considered in the plant line, are Chlorophytum Variegatum and, as a special treat, Sanseveria Laurentii, though this is more expensive than most of the house plants.

Prior to planting in the bowl, remove the existing crock material and use a little bulb fibre or similar rooting medium to fill in any spaces. Bear in mind, however, that with bowls lacking drainage holes, watering will need to be done with extra care. Always drain off any water lying in the bottom of the bowl. One of the most popular climbing plants for indoor decoration is Hedera (ivy). There are several species, and amongst the best known sorts are: Hedera Helix Cristata which has green foliage and Hedera Canariensis which has variegated leaves. As well as being grown as climbers, they will do well if allowed to trail, as from a pot in a wall bracket.

Perhaps the most popular of all indoor plants is Tradescantia. The variety Tradescantia Fluminensia Variegata, with its silvery foliage, is one of the best sorts and makes a neat graceful plant.

Plants for Window Boxes.

Many of the shorter-growing subjects used for summer bedding are also grown in window boxes. Geraniums are amongst the most popular, these being planted from pots in May. They are subjects which do well in town conditions.

The dwarf varieties of African Marigolds give a pleasing effect, the golden yellow contrasting well with blue lobelia which, trailing over the front of the box, makes a bold splash of colour.

For a spring display, polyanthus in mixed colours are very effective and some of the newer strains now available provide a wealth of colour.

Wallflowers are another possibility for spring flowering. Petunias and dwarf bedding dahlias should be borne in mind for a late summer display. For further selection, the bedding plants described in Chapter 8, will provide a choice but, for the most part, the dwarfer subjects are the more suitable. Often we can choose colours that contrast with the paintwork or the brickwork of the house and thus obtain an even brighter eye-catching display. Brilliant red Salvias, for example, show up well against a grey or fawn-coloured stone.

Plants for Hanging Baskets.

The trailing types, most popular for this purpose, include ivy-leaved geraniums, weeping (pendulous) varieties of fuchsias, begonia pendula, trailing lobelia, petunias and nasturtiums. Fuchsias are especially valuable and there are several varieties of weeping habit very suited for hanging basket work. These include Marinka, which has crimson-scarlet sepals with a red corolla and is very free flowering and Cascade which has long white sepals—with a red flush and a deep carmine-red corolla and is also very free flowering.

The wire baskets used for this purpose can be 8ins., 9ins., 10ins. or even larger in diameter, but the 10in. size makes for a very good display. Stand the empty basket on an empty flower pot and line the sides and bottom with moss, or similar material to keep the soil or compost in place. Half fill with soil; a mixture of half loam or garden soil and half well-rotted compost will give very good results. If plants are wanted in the sides of the basket, which is a good plan, set these in position and, after making suitable holes in the moss, allow the foliage and shoots to hang free. Plant the top of the basket with the selected subjects, leaving some space for watering, by having a shallow depression in the centre.

Chapter VII

The Small Greenhouse and Conservatory

for Flower Growing.

1. General Points in Management.

2. Making use of the Greenhouse for:

    Growing Pot Plants.

    Raising Bedding Plants.

    Growing Chrysanthemums.

    Taking Cuttings.

3. Use of a Conservatory for Pot Plants.

4. Some Popular Pot Plants.

5. Use of a Frame for Flower Growing.

General Points in Management.

A small greenhouse is useful in that it can be used for raising bedding plants for spring and early summer planting and, also, provide pot plants for decoration in the home through much of the year.

The winter use of a greenhouse depends on whether it is heated, and if so, by what means. It is expensive to heat a house throughout the winter, solely to grow plants for pleasure. Often, if one grows chrysanthemums in pots for November and December flowering, which entails heating, little further use may be made of the glass until propagation starts in February.

We have already touched on some of the main uses of a greenhouse, i.e. for pot plants, for raising bedding plants and for chrysanthemum-growing in the autumn and early winter. As an alternative, some pot plants may be grown for October-December flowering. Often, the main summer use of a greenhouse is for tomatoes which do not enter into our flower survey here. To deal then in more detail with each of these main subjects:

Making use of the Greenhouse.

Growing Pot Plants.—The subjects that are most easily grown in a small greenhouse are dealt with later in this chapter. Many can be raised from seed, but if one has not had much previous experience of raising these subjects it is best to start with one or two, until confidence is gained.

Some helpful points of management where one has a collection of pot and other plants in a greenhouse are as follows:

General Attention.—Where one has a batch of mixed plants, standing on a bench or staging, look them over about twice a week, if possible, and remove any dead leaves. Stir the surface of the soil, if it is very hard, and move the pots slightly about once a week to ensure balanced growth. Many plants in flower respond to better air circulation if they are stood on an empty inverted pot, of the same size. This not only shows off the flowers to best advantage but gives a better overall display.

96

Feeding.—In summer, and when plants are growing up to the flowering stage, most specimens respond to extra feeding. One of the best methods is to use liquid manure water. To obtain this, suspend a small bag full of manure in a tub or tank of water, and give it a "prod" every day. Use the liquid which results diluted to 10 parts of water, and feed the pot plants once a week with this in place of an ordinary watering.

Liquid manure not only contains most of the plant foods that are required but adds an extra "something" which gives better finish to the plants and improves the colour intensity of the flowers. Weak soot water can be given as a change, but bear in mind that this provides mostly nitrogen. It can be made in the same way as described for liquid manure.

Watering.—This causes more confusion than any other factor. For growing plants in spring and summer, more water is needed than in autumn or winter but, in either case, it is best to rely on tapping the pots daily (twice a day in hot weather) to ascertain the water requirement. Use the handle of a knife or a cotton reel on a wire handle. If the soil in the pot is dry, there will be a hollow, high-toned "ring" when the pot is tapped. If it is wet there will just be a dull "thud". In this latter case do not water.

Water, either too much or too little, is probably the cause of many pot plants being checked or even killed. Over-watering is probably the most common fault, as the effects are not so quickly apparent as under-watering, where the plant "flags" or wilts.

The following points should be borne in mind for general guidance:

1. Do not just damp the surface. If the plant needs water, soak it, fill up the pot, let the water soak away, then water again. There must always be enough space left when potting to allow for watering. This may be an inch or more, depending on the size of pot.

2. To determine need for water, tap the pot with the knuckles or a wooden mallet—a cotton reel on a cane will suffice for medium-sized pots. If the pot really "rings"

97

it is on the dry side, if there is a dull "thud" it is wet. With large pots the difference in weight between a dry plant and a wet one is worth checking.

3. Where there is a batch of pot plants, in practice one finds that perhaps a third are dry and need water, a third are really wet, needing none, and the other third will probably need checking over again later in the day.

4. In warm sunny weather it is best to look over the plants two or even three times a day.

5. The colour of the soil may, with practice, denote need for water or otherwise, but do not be misguided by the state of the top layer; it may be dry, yet the remainder of the ball of soil not in need of water.

6. If one person does the watering, it is easier than if others do it as well. One gets to know the plants and their individual requirements.

7. Weather can affect considerably the amount of water required. Tap each one if in doubt. Dull weather means less watering. Keep plants on the dry side in winter, rather than overdo the application.

8. Do not wash the soil out of the pot in watering. Use a small spout attachment on the can if it is too large, or plug the end with a piece of wood.

9. If using a hose pipe adjust the pressure according to requirements.

10. For small numbers of pots, stand a really dry plant in a bowl or bath of water and let it soak up all it needs.

11. Do not top dress or feed a dry plant, or the mixture may be too rich and damage to roots result.

12. Incorporate liquid manure in watering every 10 days or so, where necessary, to plants in growth and coming up to flower.

13. Do not be misled by a storm of rain in pots of, for example, chrysanthemums out of doors in summer. The leaves and the plants themselves shield much of the soil from rain and on checking the pots, many will often be found really dry.

14. It is impossible in general notes of this sort to deal with the watering of succulents and plants that are being dried off. The above remarks are intended as a general guide to

the treatment of the average pot plants grown, for those who have not had many pot plants before.

15. Finally, above all, do not water indiscriminately; do not water all the plants at once and water only if needed—then water well.

Potting Mixtures.—A good, general-purpose potting mixture can be made from mature, well-made compost, passed through a ⅛in. sieve, plus coarse sand, peat and loam. The proportions can be 2 parts compost, 2 parts loam and 1 part each of peat and coarse sand. Make sure that the latter is coarse, as the drainage benefit it gives to the mixture is most important.

If loam (the result of turf being stacked for 6 months or so) is unobtainable, the alternative is to use the best garden soil available. In any case, to each bucketful of potting mixture add a handful each of bone meal, hoof and horn and wood ash.

Pest Control in the Greenhouse.—There are several pests that may attack plants under glass and, under warm summer conditions especially, pests can increase very quickly. The best insurance against attack is a good growing medium combined with good management. One of the most common pests is White Fly, especially on fuchsias and pelargoniums. As a last resort and as an expedient, fumigation with D.D.T. or B.H.C. smoke cartridges may have to be done. Make sure that the cartridge or cannister used is the right size for the cubic capacity of the house (length by breadth by average height). Either of the fumigants mentioned will kill Aphides but spraying can also be done against this latter pest and the same details as given in Chapter 9 apply. Avoid such poisonous substances whenever possible, however, by correct treatment and management which will result in healthy growth.

Ventilation.—In summer, adequate ventilation must be given. For general guidance, the ventilators should be opened when the temperature reaches 60 degrees F. As temperatures increase admit maximum ventilation and, if necessary, leave the door open as well.

In winter, very little ventilation may be necessary, but on

99

fine days an air change is of great benefit and opening the ventilators on the side away from the wind may be needed. Avoid cold draughts at all times.

Summer Management.—*Some shading applied to the glass* in hot, bright, weather in summer may be needed. This will reduce the amount of water required and also minimise the risk of bright sunshine scorching the foliage. Proprietary shading products are available, for mixing with water, and applying to the roof, outside, with a syringe, knapsack sprayer or even with a brush. In hot weather, damp down the pathway, the walls and staging, to keep the house cool and to maintain humidity.

Winter Management.—If the house is just adequately heated, as with a paraffin heater, it is helpful to conserve heat by lining one side of the house inside, with polythene sheeting. Do not cover the ventilators over or, if this is done, do it separately so that normal ventilation can be given. This insulation is very helpful and should be seriously considered. The polythene can be lightly tacked on to the sash bars, or with spring clip clothes pegs if the house has metal sash bars. Polythene sheeting can be obtained from most garden sundries shops.

In hard, severe spells, extra protection may be needed for some plants, by covering them at night, with newspaper. Keep the house and plants rather dry in severe frosty spells. Growing plants should be watered only when they need it, and plants like geranium stools can be left quite dry for long periods, but not so dry that the stems shrivel.

Raising Bedding Plants.—Several subjects can be raised, in a heated greenhouse, for April and May planting. The most popular subjects are described in Chapter 8 and any of these can be raised quite easily on a small scale.

The basic requirements are some pots in which to sow the seeds and some seed boxes into which the seedlings are pricked out (transplanted). It is possible to buy seed compost for raising these subjects and for growing the plants in trays, where no compost of one's own making is yet available. Where the latter is possible, use 3 parts loam, 2 parts of compost passed through an ⅛in. sieve and 1 part of coarse sand.

The sowing is done as follows. 5in. or even 3½in. pots can be used but, assuming the former, place two or three pieces of crock (broken pot) over the drainage hole in the bottom and fill to 1in. from the top with seed sowing mixture. Level the surface and firm this with the bottom of an empty 5in. pot.

Sow the seed thinly (for guidance 40 to the square inch), and cover it by using a fine mesh sieve if available; if not, place the covering soil over the seed by hand. The depth of covering varies according to the seed but is about ⅛in. for many flower seeds. Those which are very small, almost dust-like, are barely covered.

Speaking of small seeds, bear in mind that a good way with subjects like lobelia is to sow the seeds on a sheet of white paper cut to the size of a seed tray, then pour them into the screw top from a small bottle and use this as a measure.

The method of sowing larger seeds is the same, although those which can be easily handled, such as sweet peas, may be space sown, an inch or so apart in the box. Broadly speaking, the larger seeds may be covered in the fine surface soil to a depth of about double their size. It is a good plan to water the soil an hour or two before sowing the seeds, the covering soil used after sowing being, however, of just the customary moisture content.

After sowing, water carefully with a fine rosed can, and place a sheet of glass over the top of the pot, covering this with a sheet of brown paper. Stand the pots on a bench or staging in the greenhouse.

Examine the pots for water requirement each day, and remove the glass when there are signs of germination. As soon as the seedlings are large enough to handle transplant them into a seed tray, 9 the long way and 6 across the tray. Transplant firmly but with care to avoid damage to the small stems. Make sure the compost is level and firm. Allow room for watering and fill the trays to about ¾in. from the top, with this factor in mind.

A marker should be made to facilitate pricking out. What is needed is a piece of wood 1in. thick, cut to the size of the inside dimension of the tray. Drive 54 studs in one side, equally spaced, which when pressed into the surface of the seed tray will make the positions where the seedlings are to be transplanted.

When preparing the seed trays place a ½in. layer of rotted manure or compost in the bottom. This will ensure strong, sturdy plants later. Water the seedlings in, and grow them on, best of all on a shelf, near the glass, otherwise on the bench or staging in full light.

After about 4 weeks in the greenhouse, boxes can be stood out in a cold frame, but this should be kept closed for a few days unless the weather is very warm. Then later, give ventilation by day and, after 2 weeks or so, ventilation by night. After a further two weeks, the lights can be left off and the boxes stood out under a hedge or wall for the final stages of what is called "hardening off". Throughout this period, water the plants as they need it; avoid over-watering, but do not allow any plants to flag (wilt).

Seeds of the subjects mentioned may be sown in February. This will mean that plants will be growing on under glass in March and be out in cold frames for early April. Most of these are planted out in May.

Not only will the home production of bedding plants save money (they usually cost 2/- or more for a dozen plants) but one can choose the exact type and colours required for the bedding scheme in mind, and be sure of having the plants exactly when required.

Chrysanthemums.—If one has a heated greenhouse, a few November and December flowering varieties are a great asset, not only for decoration in themselves but to provide cut flowers for the home. It is not possible here to deal with the subject in detail, but for those who would like to try a few plants for the first time, the following is a brief summary of the main operations involved.

Cuttings are taken in February or March, in a heated greenhouse. Use the shoots which arise from the old stools (plants which flowered last year). The method is as for the early flowering varieties, described in Chapter 4. When rooted, pot the cuttings singly into 4½in. pots, using equal parts of loam, compost and sand. By the end of May or early June, pot on into either 9in. or 10in. pots, which must be well crocked. Use

102

3 parts loam, 1 part rotted manure or compost and 1 part coarse grit and add to each bucketful of the resultant compost a mixture of 2ozs. bone meal, 1oz. hoof and horn and 4ozs. dry wood ash.

Stand the pots outside on a hard base and give each plant a 4ft. high cane. Take the tops out of the plants when 9ins. high, and select the best 6 or 8 shoots that arise, removing the rest. Tie the shoots to the canes, water regularly, and remove any side buds so as to leave only one flower bud at the end of each of the main shoots. Remove any surplus growths or side shoots, and feed with weak liquid manure, once a week. It is best to bring the plants indoors in late September, before frosts threaten. After housing, continue disbudding, watering and feeding. Give frost-free conditions, this being important, but grow the plants as cool as possible, giving maximum ventilation compatible with outside conditions.

Some suitable varieties for this method of growing are:

November Flowering.—Loveliness, pink, and any of the Loveliness sports, e.g. Apricot, White or Lilac Loveliness; Worthing Success, pink; Balcombe Perfection, red or Symbol, orange.

December Flowering.—The Favourite, white; Red Favourite; Imperial Pink, and Fred Shoesmith, white.

All these are decorative varieties, not the large flowered exhibition sorts, and are but a very few of the many varieties listed in chrysanthemum catalogues for December flowering. All can be recommended for the newcomer to chrysanthemum growing.

Taking Cuttings.—Reference has been made to this method of propagation in respect of many subjects, e.g. geraniums (see Fig. 11), fuchsias and chrysanthemums. It should be borne in mind that a small propagating frame, even a small wooden box with a glass top, will provide good facilities for rooting a wide range of cuttings. Such a small frame, on the bench in the warmest part of the greenhouse, will provide the "close" conditions which enable cuttings to root quickly.

For many cuttings a good rooting medium is equal parts of sharp (fine) sand and a fine grade peat. Pure sand can be used, and vermiculite is also a very good rooting medium. The propagating frame should be very well drained and coarse material can be placed in the bottom to provide this condition. The rooting medium should be about 6ins. thick, or a little less.

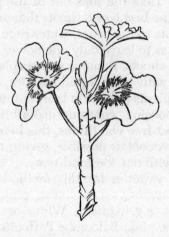

Fig. 11.—Prepared cutting of Geranium

Generally speaking, most cuttings should be several inches in length, bear two or three pairs of leaves and terminate in a growing shoot. Fig. 11 clearly shows this, and also how to prepare a cutting of a semi-hard stemmed plant, such as the geranium.

It will be noted that the slanting cut at the base of the cutting is made just below a joint, or the place where the leaves have been growing, the leaves being trimmed off up the stem for the half of the cutting that is to be inserted. If the slanting cut is made at some distance below the joint, that part will rot off, and possibly the rot may continue, while the rootlets that ought to form from underneath the joint will not appear.

All cuttings should be inserted firmly, and care should be taken not to over-water. Small batches can be rooted quite easily in pots, the cuttings being inserted around the edge where the better aeration makes for quicker rooting.

104

Root Cuttings.—Mention has been made of this method of propagation with phlox, where new plants free of eel worm are required. Another subject which can be propagated by this method is gaillardia. The roots are selected in winter and cut into portions 3ins. long. They should be inserted upright, in a cold frame, with the thickest end cut flat, and this be kept at the same level as the rooting medium in the frame.

Use of a Conservatory for Pot Plants.

A conservatory may be a lean-to greenhouse. It is usually unheated, which means that it is chiefly the spring, summer and autumn flowering subjects that are used to make up a display. If one is fortunate enough to have both greenhouse and conservatory, then the latter can be used for the plants just coming into flower and in full bloom. The fullest possible use should be made of spring flowering bulbs, narcissi and daffodils. For summer, bear in mind fuchsias and pelargoniums, with cyclamen and chrysanthemums the highlights for the autumn. The same general principles of management apply as given earlier in this chapter.

If a conservatory is being used only in the summer months a very colourful display can be obtained by raising annuals in pots. Most of the shorter or medium height subjects used for bedding purposes are suitable and, if one has no greenhouse and must purchase all one's plants, some of the following subjects should be borne in mind for growing under these circumstances. They may be bought ex boxes, or in pots.

Petunias are especially colourful, and some of the newer hybrids, such as Glitters and Red Satin, are very suitable for growing in this way. These can usually be purchased in pots. The climbing plant Ipoinoea Heavenly Blue, will give pleasure also. The Camellia Flowered Balsam should be included, as there is a wide range of colours, and the plants are very suitable for growing in pots. Cockscomb, especially the crimson variety, is also a good subject for this purpose, as is Salvia Blaze of Fire. Some of these may be in 3in. paper pots when purchased and should be potted into 3½in. ordinary clay pots, on receipt. A small supply of potting compost may need to be purchased for this purpose, and J.I.P.1 will be suitable, or if available, use 3 parts loam, 1 part compost and 1 part of sand.

If one is starting from scratch, and has a greenhouse, and an empty conservatory, then all or any of the above can be raised from seed to give a colourful display at reasonable cost.

Some bedding plants from boxes, which can be used for a cold conservatory include lobelia, for the front of the display, dwarf nasturtiums, Ice Plant (mesembryanthemum), dwarf double French marigolds, nemesia, especially the dwarf varieties, and any of the shorter varieties of antirrhinums. These can be grown singly in 3½in. pots to begin with and be moved on to 5in. pots as necessary. All these annuals are discarded after flowering, but with choice of subjects and spreading the purchase of plants over a long period, one can have a lengthy display of colour through the summer months.

If one has a greenhouse, or if the conservatory is heated in winter, some pot subjects (i.e. perennials) that can be purchased for summer flowering and which can be kept for future use, are: fuchsia, pelargonium, geranium, heliotrope, coleus (for its coloured foliage) asparagus fern and tuberous rooted begonias.

Some of the taller subjects may need staking with thin canes and the same attention to watering and feeding, as described under "General Management of Pot Plants", will be required.

Some Popular Pot Plants.

Coleus.—The vari-coloured foliage of this plant makes it an attractive subject for pots, especially in spring and summer. It is, however, a plant which must be kept out of draughts, as the leaves may fall if it is given conditions it does not like in this respect. This is one of the most common troubles. Over-watering will also give rise to leaf drop, and it is best to make sure that the crocking of any pot containing coleus is adequate for best results. Compost must also be well drained to allow free passage of water.

If re-potting is needed, use a rich compost—if possible: 3 parts loam, 2 parts sieved compost and 1 part of coarse grit. In re-potting, do not pot too firmly.

Coleus can be raised from seed, but this gives rise to a

percentage of green or greenish foliage types, and these should be discarded, keeping only the reddish ones or those which appear promising as far as leaf colour is concerned.

The usual method of propagation is by cuttings. These are best taken as follows: select a shoot 3ins. long from the side of the plant, preferably from the lower part, leave the tip intact and neatly remove the lowest pair of leaves. Cut through the leaf joint and insert firmly in sand, or half sand and half compost in a 3in. pot. Water carefully as required.

If long shoots at the top of a plant are trimmed back to keep the shape neat and well balanced, the tips of such shoots can also be used for cuttings.

Chrysanthemums.—Some of the dwarf varieties are very suitable as pot plants and the yellow, Jante Wells, is probably the best known. It is best to grow these in 5in. pots, and to plan for a September and October display. Cuttings are taken in April, rooted in the same way as described in Chapter 4, and, when ready, moved into 3in. pots.

When the plants are well rooted in these, pot them on to the 5in. size. A good potting mixture for this purpose is 2 parts loam, 1 part compost, 1 part peat and 1 part coarse sand. To each bucketful of the mixture add a handful each of bone meal, hoof and horn and wood ash.

If Jante Wells is being grown, when the plants are about 5ins. high the tops should be taken out, to encourage side shoots and give bushy compact growth. The plants should be hardened off and then stood out on a hard base for the summer months. They need to be spaced out, as growth develops. Pay careful attention to watering throughout, and feed with liquid manure every 10 to 14 days. These subjects should be taken indoors in September, as the buds show colour, and grown under cool, well ventilated conditions.

There is a group of varieties called the Dwarf Lilliputs that are very suitable for this type of cultivation, all being 8 to 12ins. high and of compact, neat habit. None of these need stopping or staking. These varieties are very free flowering; some that can be recommended are: Cadet, red; Doris, lilac; Isis, rose pink; Osiris, rosy-mauve, and Pimpernel, chestnut red. They make a valuable contribution to an autumn display.

Cinerarias.—These need heat through the winter months and are grown chiefly for spring display. The dwarf multiflora varieties are easiest for small batches. Seed is sown in June, and the seedlings can be pricked out into 3in. pots. These plants must have good drainage and, when potting finally into 5in. pots, make sure that enough crocks are laid in position. For the autumn and winter, cool but frost free conditions are necessary.

These bold and colourful pot plants make an attractive display but demand rather more than usual care and attention in their management. They call for extra care with watering, in that too much causes damage to the roots. Often when the leaves are seen to be flagging, it is assumed that the compost is dry and more water is given. As a result, the plant can be killed very quickly.

Before watering is done it is essential to tap the pots sharply to ascertain moisture requirements. Only give water when the compost is dry, i.e. when the pot rings on being tapped. If in doubt delay watering for the time being.

Apart from the root troubles mentioned earlier one of the chief problems can be aphides, and these pests are quickly attracted to the soft tips of the plants. Regular spraying with derris preparations may be essential to keep these plants clean of such pests.

I find that I can do best with these plants by growing them in a very sharply-drained compost and I like the following mixture best of all: 3 parts loam, 1 part coarse grit, and 2 parts compost.

Do not start feeding plants until the buds are well developed as too much, too soon, can cause an excessive amount of foliage to be produced at the expense of the flower.

Cyclamen.—This is one of the most popular pot plants for September to Christmas flowering. Many colours are available, but pink and red varieties are the most popular. The plants need a long growing season, seed is sown in August of one year, for flowering during September to December the next year. Sow the seeds in 5in. pots under glass. When the young plants are 3ins. high, which will be in early autumn, transfer them to 3in. pots, in a mixture of 2 parts loam, 2 parts compost and 1 part sand.

In spring move the plants into 5in. pots, in which they will flower. Use the same mixture for this potting, but place a 1in. layer of rotted compost in the bottom, over the crocks. Good drainage is essential for cyclamen. For the summer months stand the pots out in cold frames, paying careful attention to watering.

Cyclamen will respond to liquid manure feeds throughout this period, and until the buds show colour.

Bring the plants into the greenhouse in September, before the first frosts threaten. Grow under cool conditions, space out the pots so that they are not crowded and avoid over-watering.

Fuchsias.—These colourful plants flower through the summer months, and there is a wealth of varieties, of which the double white and pink Ballet Girl is popular, also the double pink Fascination.

Propagation is by cuttings which can be taken in early spring, using new side shoots 3ins. long, removing the lower leaves, and inserting firmly in a ½ sand and ½ peat compost. Pot up into 3in. pots when rooted, later into 5in. pots for flowering. Staking is needed for most varieties. Liquid manure feeds are of especial benefit and should be given every 10 to 14 days in summer.

Make certain that this subject is kept out of draughts, which can cause the flowers to drop. Another reason for this same trouble is uneven temperature conditions, i.e. extreme variations, and careful attention to this point can prevent disappointment.

When the flush of flowers is over, the main branches (shoots) can be pinched back to encourage new growth, and to keep the general habit of the plant neat and well furnished. Remove about a third of the shoots in each case.

Watering should be attended to regularly; never allow plants to flag, as this, too, can cause flowers to drop. When water is required, fill up the space available, more than once if necessary, and then leave, until the compost dries to the stage when the pot "rings" if rapped with the knuckles.

These colourful and attractive plants repay careful attention to the above details.

Polyanthus.—For an easy to grow pot plant, polyanthus should be tried. If a few plants are lifted during mild weather, and potted into a pot size just larger than the width of the ball of roots, they can be relied upon to give some flowers indoors, so long as they are given cool conditions, not over-watered, or kept in too damp an atmosphere.

When lifting a few plants in autumn select those with ample crowns, that is the central fleshy portion, and not over much leaf. Remove any brown outer leaves cleanly. When potting, use a light well-drained compost, of 3 parts loam, 1 part sand and 1 part of leaf mould. Pot fairly firmly, making sure that the pots are well crocked, as free drainage is important with these plants.

Such plants will make a useful Mothering Sunday gift. If three or four pots are grown, if possible of different colours, an appropriate choice can be made to suit individual preference. Do not try to hurry the plants when they approach the flowering stage, as they do not respond to over-warm conditions.

Pelargoniums.—These are valuable plants for summer flowering and cuttings can be taken from mature plants in September, or spring. Insert these around the edge of a 5in. pot in a sandy compost. Pot up when rooted, singly, into 3in. pots, in J.I.P.1 and later when the pots are filled with roots into 5in. pots, using J.I.P.2 or 3 parts loam, 1 part compost and 1 part of sand. Feed with liquid manure until the flowers open. A popular pink variety is Carisbrook, and, if only one variety is grown, this can be the choice.

It is essential that these plants be given frost-proof conditions in winter. They need very little watering during these months, and the shoots can be cut back in autumn, or early spring, to encourage bushy, well-shaped plants.

Tuberous Begonias.—These colourful subjects are grown from corms, which are started into growth in a tray of peat, in the greenhouse in March (or earlier if desired). When they have made roots about 2ins. long, move each plant into a 3½in.

pot, and use 2 parts compost, 1 part loam and 1 part sand for the potting mixture. Later, move on to 5in. pots containing the same mixture, but place a 1in. layer of compost or rotted manure over the crocks first. A small stake is needed, and early flowers should be pinched off, to improve the size in those which follow. Feed weekly with liquid manure when flowers show colour or use soot water one week and liquid manure the next. Begonias show good response to this type of feeding.

Use of a Frame for Flower Growing.

Frames.—We have already mentioned the use of a cold frame for the hardening off of bedding plants in early spring. If geraniums are being raised, then a frame plays a useful part for these subjects also, prior to their being planted out of doors.

In autumn, sweet peas can be raised very well in pots or boxes, in a frame, but guard against mice which are partial to the seeds. In spring, the early flowering chrysanthemums will need to spend a few weeks in the frame before being planted outside, as will the dahlias. The summer use of a cold frame may be mostly for vegetables but pot plants, such as cyclamen, will spend some of their time in such conditions.

Temporary protection for plants in pots or boxes can be given by using polythene lights, i.e. sheets of thick polythene tacked on to light wooden frames. This material is especially useful for the last stages of "hardening off" of bedding plants.

The accent is on spring, as far as the use of a cold frame is concerned, with flower-growing in mind. If a frame can be set aside for propagation purposes, so much the better. Use a sandy compost, topped off with a 3in. layer of ½ sand and ½ peat which should come up to within 6ins. of the glass. Some cuttings that can be struck very well in this mixture are delphinium, lupins and scabious amongst herbaceous plants, and, although they are not dealt with in this book, many soft wood shrub cuttings in the summer months.

If a new frame is required, bear in mind that a Dutch light, that is one with a single sheet of glass, admits the maximum amount of light.

Chapter VIII

Plants to Grow.

1. A Selection of 22 Herbaceous Plants.

2. A Selection of 20 Hardy Annuals.

3. Spring Flowering Bedding Plants.

4. Summer Flowering Bedding Plants.

5. A Selection of 20 Good Subjects for the Rock Garden.

Where new plants are being purchased, a choice can be made from the following selected subjects, brief details of cultivation being given in each case. A wider selection can be made from nurserymens' catalogues, but it is always a good plan to take note of any plants that "catch the eye" at shows, or in parks, or especially in friends' gardens (where it may be possible to obtain a "root" in autumn or winter), and to jot down their names at the time so that they are not forgotten.

Achillea.—These plants do well in sandy soils and especially hot, dry, soils. They mostly reach 2½ to 3ft. in height and flower in July and August. A well-known variety is Coronation Gold, which has silvery foliage (always a useful contrast in a border) and yellow flowers. Propagation can be by seed, or by division of mature plants in autumn or spring.

Alstromeria.—Often called Peruvian Lilies, these are very colourful subjects for summer flowering. There are orange and red varieties, and all grow about 3ft. high. They are rather slow to establish themselves and prefer a light to medium, well-drained soil. Plants can be raised from seed, or established crowns can be lifted and the roots planted, preferably in spring. Cover the pieces of root 4ins. deep in medium-heavy soils, 6ins. deep on light soils. A popular variety is Dover Orange. Alstromeria are also very popular for cutting purposes, being attractive and long lasting.

Anemone Japonica.—These herbaceous plants have an especial value in early autumn, as there is less choice of flowering subjects at this time. They will do quite well in shade and even in cold, exposed, positions. A well-known variety is A. Japonica Alba, which has white flowers and reaches a height of 3ft. Queen Charlotte is a double pink variety which is 2½ft. in height. Propagation can be by seed, and also by division which is best done in spring. Once established these plants can be left undisturbed until they become so overcrowded that lifting and division are essential.

Anchusa Italica.—This makes a brilliant display in June, the blue flowers being of vivid colouring. A good variety is Morning Glory, which is 4ft. high. Set several plants in a group, as they are rather spreading in habit. Anchusa has a fleshy root stock, does not divide very readily, but is easily raised from seed. Plants should be replaced every three years for best results. They are useful subjects for filling up a large area to good effect.

Asters (Michaelmas Daisies).—These well-known plants are indispensable for autumn flowering. All are readily propagated by division, which should be done every other year to maintain the quality of the flowers. If the plants stay down longer they deteriorate. Do not grow the taller varieties unless there is ample room for them. There are many different sorts, the following being a selection which can be relied upon: Blue Gem, 4ft., blue, semi-double flowers, late; Eventide, 3ft., violet blue, semi double; Prosperity, 4ft. heather pink, double flowers; Winston Churchill, 2½ft., claret red, and Tapestry, 2½ft., pink with double flowers.

There are also many dwarf varieties, all 1ft. high, which are useful for September and October flowering. They include: Blue Bouquet, blue and violet; Lilac Time, lilac-pink; Margaret Rose, pink, double flowered, and Audrey, lavender-blue. These are particularly valuable for the front of a border but, like the taller sorts, are best lifted and divided every second year.

Astilbe.—These plants, which resemble Spiraea, have finely divided foliage and plumes of flowers which are borne in July. It is possible to raise some varieties from seed but the named varieties are divided. These plants do not do well in poor, dry soils. A good selection of varieties is: Etna, 1½ft., crimson; Red Sentinel, 2½ft, red, and Salmon Queen, 2½ft., shell pink. These plants respond very well to a mulch of leaf mould or compost during the growing season, treatment which should be repeated every year.

Aquilega.—Usually known as Columbines, these well-known flowers provide a wealth of colour in May and June.

They are easily raised from seed, and there are now many colourful varieties, the McKana Giant hybrids being especially good. Aquilegas will do quite well in a shaded position and should always be borne in mind for such a site, the choice for such a situation being rather limited.

Delphiniums.—These tall subjects are outstanding where there is space for them. They provide many shades of blue for summer flowering. They need rich soil, with an ample supply of compost, and should be planted in autumn, if possible, as they start into growth early in spring. Slugs often attack the foliage, and the crowns can be protected with a layer of ashes in the winter, with this factor in mind. Seed of several good strains is available and will provide suitable plants for herbaceous border planting. Named varieties include Blue Gown, Nell Gwynne, semi-double, mauve, and C. F. Langdon, blue with a black centre. All are tall growing and need support from canes or stakes, to which the shoots should be tied securely, especially in exposed positions.

Doronicum.—This is one of the earliest plants to flower, the yellow daisy like blooms being borne in April. The plants are 3ft. high and the fleshy roots can be divided in autumn. Some varieties can be raised from seed. A good named variety is Harpur Crewe, of which a bold clump can be relied upon to give some welcome colour in spring. It is a plant that responds especially well to a mulch of compost in late winter.

Erigeron.—These are easy to grow, summer-flowering plants, which can be readily propagated by division, in autumn, or raised from seed. All are near to 2ft. in height. Some good named varieties are : Dignity, violet; Unity, pink; Sincerity, mauve-violet, and Wuppertal, pale violet. This latter sort is very free flowering and deserves a place in every border. It is best to lift and divide established plants every second year, otherwise the flowers decrease in size and quality.

Gaillardia Grandiflora.—These are brilliant flowers, mostly red, orange and yellow, for July display. Wirral Flame is a particularly bright red variety. Propagation can be by seed for many varieties, whilst the fleshy roots lend themselves to root cuttings. Division in October can also be done. Most Gaillardias are about 3ft. high, and do best on the lighter types of soil but, even on heavy clay, will respond to generous compost applications. The flowers are especially colourful and very useful for cutting.

Helenium.—These plants do well even in dry poor soils, and the colourful, daisy-like flowers are borne in July and August. Plants should be divided frequently, if possible every year, for best results. Seed of some varieties is available and plants are easily raised by this means. Good named sorts are Moerheim Beauty, 3ft., with red flowers (a "must" for the herbaceous border), and The Bishop, which is rather later flowering and has yellow blooms with a brown centre.

Hemerocallis.—These colourful subjects often called Day Lilies, make a very bright display and have a long flowering season. They are easy of culture and should be included in every new border. Some good varieties are: Amber, 2½ft., pale yellow, June to July; Gold Dust, 2ft., golden yellow, May to June, and Radiant, 3ft., orange, June to August. Propagation is by division in October, or seed is available of some varieties. If possible, choose a sunny site for these colourful subjects.

Iris (Bearded).—These subjects have a rather short flowering season but one or two plants should be included in every border. They require a position in full sun and there must be ample lime or old mortar rubble in the soil. Plant so that the upper surface of the rhizome is exposed. The flowering season is June. A good violet variety is Sir Michael, whilst Blue Rhythm and Corrida are colourful blue sorts. Golden Flare is apricot, and Senlac is red and purple. The planting season is March, July or October but, if possible, this should be done after flowering.

Lupins.—These colourful and popular plants should be raised afresh from seed each year, or every other year, to keep a continuity of supply. The Russell Lupins are well known, and some named varieties include Canary Bird, yellow;

117

Venus, salmon red and crimson; Fire Glow, orange; Heather Glow, purple, and Charmaine, buff orange. All reach a height of about 3ft. If one saves seed from one's own plants, mixed colours will result, i.e. the colours sown will not come true, but satisfactory plants for general purposes can be obtained. Lupins are at their best in June and July and no border is complete without a few plants of these popular subjects.

Paeonies.—These, often called the aristocrats of the border, are certainly deserving of this title. The plants take a few years to become really established and can then stay undisturbed for a long period. When planting, make sure that the crowns are not covered more than 2ins. as a greater depth can cause failure to flower. The double paeonies are not raised from seed but established plants can be divided, the best planting time being September and October. Most varieties are 2½ft. high and a choice of named sorts can be made from the following, all of which are first class: Sarah Bernhardt, an apple-blossom pink; Karl Rosefield, crimson; Kelways Glorious, white; Laura Derwent, cream; Felix Crousse, crimson; President Wilson, pink, and Mons. Jule Elie, rose pink.

Paeonies benefit considerably from a manure or compost mulch and a generous application should be given each spring, this being spread evenly over the area between the plants. The common red paeony often seen in gardens is P. Officinalis, which flowers in May, rather sooner than the varieties described above. A few paeonies are a "must" for the new border; although the plants may cost a little more than many subjects, the extra expenditure is well worth while.

Phlox.—These very brightly-coloured subjects are at their best in June, July and August. New plants should be obtained from a good source, to be free of eel worm. Some good varieties are Blue Moon, Dresden China, shell pink; Prunella, rosy violet; Signal, salmon orange, and Rosebella, deep rose. All are about 3ft. high. Healthy plants can be propagated by division in autumn or spring. Propagation by root cuttings is dealt with in Chapter 7.

Pyrethrum.—This is a particularly attractive subject for

118

June flowering, the red and pink varieties being especially colourful. Established plants can be lifted and divided after flowering, in July. The "splits" or divisions should be about 2ins. across. Some good varieties are Kelways Glorious, red; E. M. Robinson, pink, and Salmon Beauty. All grow about 3ft. high, and are a "must" for the herbaceous border. They are also especially good for cutting.

Plants can also be raised from seed, but the colours may be varied; if seed is saved from say a red variety the resulting plants may be different. Nevertheless this method of propagation should be used for building up a stock of plants quickly, at least expense.

Scabious.—The best-known variety is Clive Greaves, which gives a pleasing soft lavender blue display from July to October. Spring planting is best for this subject, and an adequate supply of lime in the soil is essential. It is of compact habit, 2½ to 3ft. tall, and one of the best plants that can be obtained for the herbaceous border. It is also a very popular flower for cutting, lasting well in water, and with a good length of stem.

Tritoma (Kniphofia).—The "Red Hot Pokers" are popular subjects for June to August flowering. Some varieties that should be grown include Red Chief, 4ft. high, flowering in August, and Royal Standard, also 4ft. high, which blooms very freely from July to September. Its flower spikes are half orange-red, and half lemon-yellow. Both these plants do well under a wide range of soil conditions. Propagation is by division in autumn or spring, or some varieties can be raised from seed.

Trollius.—The "Globe Flowers" as they are often called are useful for giving colour in May, and will do well in damp soil. The most striking varieties are: Etna, which is deep orange, 3ft. high, and Brilliant, also 3ft. with a dark orange colouring. Established clumps can be divided in autumn. If plants are being raised from seed, grow the variety Ledebouri, Golden Queen, which is very free-flowering, and easily propagated from seed. These are particularly valuable plants for a heavy soil.

119

Veronica Teucrium.—One of the dwarf varieties, such as Royal Blue, which is 1ft. high, will do well in the front of the border and give a bold display in June. The gentian blue flowers are strikingly colourful. Propagation is by division in autumn.

In conclusion, the reader is referred to Fig. 12, a suggested plan for a new herbaceous border.

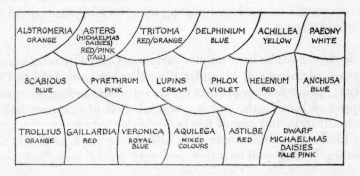

Fig. 12.—Plan of a new herbaceous border incorporating some of the subjects described in Chapter 8

A Selection of 20 Hardy Annuals.

There is a selection of hardy annuals that may be sown direct where they are to flower and, to help the reader make a suitable choice, the following subjects are listed as being especially appropriate. The details of height will serve as an indication of the position to sow, i.e., tall subjects at the back of the border, dwarf varieties in the front.

Alonsoa.—This is 2ft. high, a bright scarlet, and makes a striking display. The variety usually grown is A. Warscewiczii.

Anagallis.—The Pimpernel, is very useful for edging purposes as it is only 6ins. high. There are scarlet and blue varieties, and all do well in an open sunny position.

120

Anchusa.—The variety A. Capensis Blue Bird is very colourful and its indigo blue flowers make a vivid show. It is 18ins. high and a "must" for the annual border, being an outstanding plant.

Bartonia Aurea.—On very sandy soils or those that dry out rapidly (as when one is starting up on a poor unmanured soil) this is a very useful plant. The flowers are yellow, producing a mass of colour. Height 18ins.

Calendula.—This is one of the easiest flowers to grow of all the annuals. Best quality flowers are obtained in soils well enriched with compost, for the blooms "come single" in poor conditions. Orange Cockade is a good variety, and Radio is another of the same colour. The height reached is 18ins. in both cases. For covering a rough patch, quickly, these plants are especially valuable, and can be sown broadcast for this purpose.

Clarkia.—A packet of mixed colours will give a bright display, and the variety Fantasy, double mixed, gives a colourful effect. Their height is 2ft. Make sure that these plants are thinned out to give them ample room; 12 to 15ins. apart is not too much and the quality of flowers will be much improved as a result.

Chrysanthemum (Annual).—The Coronarium varieties are 2ft. tall and if a packet of mixed colours is sown, a bold display is ensured. These plants do well under a wide range of soil conditions, are amongst the easiest to grow, and are another useful subject for covering a piece of rough ground, to give a quick effect.

Eschscholtzia.—This is a plant for hot dry conditions, as it will do well even in these circumstances. The orange varieties are of especially vivid colouring, Orange King being a good one, but a packet of mixed colours will give a bright splash of orange, yellow, bronze and carmine.

Gaillardia.(Annual).—The variety Picta, which is orange

121

red and yellow, is very colourful and about 1ft. high. It is useful for cutting and can be relied upon for a bold display in the front of the border.

Godetia.—There are tall and dwarf varieties, both types of which are available in a wide range of colours. The reds and pinks are especially striking and make one of the most attractive subjects for the annual border. Thin out these plants so that they are not overcrowded.

Gypsophila Elegans.—Some white flowers always lend contrast to others of brighter colours, and a bold patch of Gypsophila Elegans Alba should be included in the border. The plants reach 18ins. high. The red and pink varieties are also very suitable.

Larkspur.—For the back of the border, these 3ft. tall subjects will give a good display, either in mixed colours or in blue, pink or red separately. The site for these plants should have a little extra compost, if possible, as they respond to better than average conditions. There is also a dwarf variety, 12ins. high with double flowers, of very neat habit.

Lavatera Loveliness.—This plant is a "must". The pink mallow type flowers are outstanding. Sow at the back of the border, as these subjects are 2½ to 3ft. tall. They are very free flowering and no annual border should be without a bold group of this colourful variety.

Linaria.—These are easy-to-grow plants, light in habit, and in a very wide range of colours. A packet of mixed varieties will ensure a vivid splash of colour and either the Maroccana Hybrids, 15ins. tall, can be grown, or, for the front of the border, Fairy Bouquet, which reaches 8ins. high.

Linum.—Both blue and red varieties are good for the annual border and flower in profusion. Height 15ins.

Nasturtium.—The Tom Thumb varieties are very good for the front of the border, being 9 to 12ins. high. Empress of

India, with dark foliage and crimson scarlet flowers is strikingly colourful. These are also good plants for a poor soil; indeed, too rich a soil can give excess foliage at the expense of flowers.

Phacelia Campanularia.—This is another plant for the front of the annual border, being 9ins. high. Its gentian blue flowers make it one of the subjects that must be grown and the intensity of the colouring alone makes it a plant well worth having.

Scabious (Annual).—As these plants are 2 to 3ft. tall, a position at the back of the border is needed. Here again mixed colours may be grown in the same bed, or a separate colour, red, purple or pink, be used to give effect. These plants are actually biennials but are best treated as annuals.

Sweet Sultan.—This is available in a wide range of colour, and is an easy subject to grow. It is 18ins. tall and also useful for cutting.

Viscaria.—This is another "easy-to-grow" plant, light in habit, and 15ins. high. It is available in blue and pink shades but a packet of mixed colours is best for the annual border.

Many varieties of flower seeds can be obtained from certain specialist seedsmen who raise organically-grown plants to provide the seed.

A *Child's* Garden.

Children usually like to see results quickly. For this reason, a few varieties of annuals should be provided. Some of the easiest to grow, and which flower in a short time, are: Calendula; Linum; Linaria, and Viscaria. Some seeds of these subjects can be mixed up together, and the whole be sown on one patch or area, to provide a colourful display.

Spring-Flowering Bedding Plants.

Brompton Stocks.—These do not always come through the winter very well but can be tried on the lighter, well-drained types of soil, in sheltered areas. Seed is sown in May or June, and plants transplanted 6ins. by 6ins. on a spare plot, until September, when they are set out where they are to flower, being spaced 10ins. apart. They reach a height of 15 to 18ins. and do best where there is ample lime in the soil. Popular varieties are White Lady; Empress Elizabeth, carmine; Queen Astrid, crimson, and Zephyr, lavender.

Double Daisies.—The Double Red varieties are most popular but pink or crimson should also be considered. These perennials are often treated as biennials, being dug up after flowering and composted. Varieties with quilled petals, such as Etna, are also colourful and valuable subjects for spring flowering.

Myosotis. Forget-me-Not.—One of the best varieties is Royal Blue, which is 12ins. high, but for a low growing type use the dwarf strain, which is only 6ins. tall. In sheltered areas, the variety Blue Bird will do well; it flowers sooner than other sorts and is 15ins. high. There is also a carmine pink variety, called Carmine King, which makes a contrast to the usual blue colours of these plants.

Pansies.—The winter-flowering varieties will give some flowers throughout a mild winter and can be obtained in separate shades such as yellow and blue, or as "mixed". For spring flowering good varieties are: Crimson Queen, Black Prince or Coronation Gold; for a striking display mixed colours will give good results. Englemans Giant is a very good strain which can be sown in May or June for flowering the following year, or be raised under glass in February to give blooms in early summer. Pansies are particularly useful for edging purposes.

Polyanthus.—This is one of the most valuable subjects for a spring display. To obtain plants for putting out in beds or borders (or window boxes) in September or October, one has to plan well ahead. If seed is sown thinly in rows in a cold frame in July, the plants can stay there until the next spring. Then plant them out on a spare border, 12ins. by 6ins., in semi-shade if possible. Give them a generous layer of compost, worked into the top few inches of soil before planting. No plant responds better to this treatment, a cool root run being essential. Grow them on through the summer, until required for lifting and replanting in the autumn.

Sowings can be made in a heated glasshouse in March, and plants raised in boxes for hardening off in a cold frame in May, then planted out of doors as described above. Established plants can be divided after flowering has ceased, and the divisions planted out for the summer, also as described above. Use only the strongest plants for division. Best quality flowers, on a good length of stem are obtained from seed sown afresh each year.

Sweet William.—These plants are June flowering and are particularly valuable at that time. Pink Beauty is outstanding, being a striking salmon pink. The Auricula-Eyed sorts, in mixed colours, are also colourful. These are about 1½ft. high, but there is also a dwarf type, only 9ins. tall, useful as an edging, available in pink shades or mixed colours. Wee Willie is an annual variety, 6ins. high, often grown on the annual border, especially in the front, as an edging.

Wallflowers.—The red sorts are very popular, of which Blood Red should be included in the list of varieties to grow. A good contrast will be produced by Cloth of Gold, which is a deep golden yellow. A rich shade of ruby is provided by Ellen Wilmott, whilst Vulcan is one of the best crimson varieties. One bed of an early variety, such as Early Flowering Vulcan, should also be included to lengthen the display.

Summer-Flowering Bedding Plants.

Ageratum.—This is used as an edging plant but is not so popular as either alyssum or lobelia. The chief varieties are Dwarf Blue, which is 9ins. high and should be spaced at 8ins., and Little Blue Star, 3ins. high, which can be planted at 4in. spacing.

Alyssum.—Another popular plant for edging. The best varieties are Little Dorritt, white, which is 4ins. high, and should be planted 6ins. apart, Lilac Queen, which is the same height and can be planted at similar spacing. Sweet Alyssum, white, is 9ins. high, and needs to be planted 8 to 9ins. apart. These plants are often planted alternately with Lobelia, to give a contrasting effect.

Antirrhinums.—There are several types, from the tall varieties which reach 3ft. in height, down to the very dwarf types which are 4 to 6ins. high, and useful for the front of a bed or border. One of the most popular groups, however, is the Intermediate, which is 15ins. tall and includes many well coloured and attractive varieties, such as: Nelrose, pink; Guardsman, scarlet; Fire King, orange-scarlet, and Eclipse, crimson. Plant these varieties 9 to 10ins. apart.

In areas where Antirrhinum Rust is troublesome, some of the rust-resistant varieties, such as Wisely Golden Fleece and Pink Freedom, should be grown. All are 12ins. high, and should be planted 10 to 12ins. apart. A new introduction are the Double Hybrids, which are 2ft. high, and available in a wide colour range. Antirrhinums, one of the most popular bedding plants, often form the nucleus of summer bedding displays.

Asters.—The Ostrich Plume varieties, which are double and 1½ft. high, are popular for bedding. Many colours are available and plants should be given 9 to 12ins. of space. Asters do best on light to medium soils, for on the heavy types some trouble may be experienced with "damping off" and "black leg". Do not plant until mid May, or later in cold areas, and make sure that the site is well drained. The Lilliput types make a pleasing contrast.

Dahlias.—The Coltness Hybrids, useful for providing a late summer display, are available in a good colour range. They are 2ft. high, and should be planted 10 to 12ins. apart. There is a wide range of dwarf bedding types available and for diversity of colour in early autumn there is little to equal them.

Few plants respond better to generous compost applications worked into the site before planting.

French Marigolds.—The dwarf double varieties are useful for edging, when planted 6ins. apart. Popular varieties are Petite Gold, and Petite Orange. Taller varieties such as Mahogany Red, 9ins. tall, and Golden Ball, are useful for beds or borders.

Geraniums.—If plants in 3in. or 3½in. pots are purchased, late May is the safest time for planting; if specimens are put out earlier, frost damage may result. Plant 12ins. apart. Popular varieties are: Paul Crampel: Gustav Emich; King of Denmark and Birkdale Gem. For edging, the varieties with variegated foliage should be used, such as Chelsea Gem or Flower of Spring. If plants are being grown, take cuttings 4 to 5ins. long in September, in 5in. pots in a mixture of half sand and half soil; insert the cuttings firmly around the edge of the pot, 1½ins. apart. Water sparingly, and keep free of frost over winter. Pot up into 3in. pots in February, in a light sandy mixture and harden off thoroughly before planting out.

Lobelia.—This is useful as an edging plant for the front of beds and borders. Most varieties are 4 to 6ins. high. It is very colourful and the popular varieties are: Cambridge Blue; Dark Blue, and Royal Purple. The planting distance should be 6ins., and the fact that Lobelia gives a good contrast to pink or orange flowers, should be borne in mind.

Nemesia.—This is a very colourful, easy to grow subject, and a wide range of colours is available in the large-flowered types, which are 12ins. high. There are also dwarf hybrid varieties, 8 to 10ins. high. Plant 9ins. apart in each case. A bed of mixed colours will make an attractive display. Nemesia is one of the quickest subjects to give a show of colour. The first flowers should be cut off, when they go over, to encourage the plants to "break" and flower again.

Petunia.—The commonest groups are the ordinary single-bedding Petunia, and the large-flowered single varieties, which are available in a wide range of colour. Their height is 1½ft. Plant 12ins. apart. There are, however, many attractive new hybrids which should be grown in preference to the ordinary types although, if the plants are purchased, they are more expensive. Some varieties to be recommended are: Glitters, red and white, 9ins. high, and Red Satin, vivid scarlet red, which is of dwarf habit and has very large flowers. These latter varieties should be planted 9ins. apart.

Phlox Drummondi.—This is a colourful subject and the large-flowered varieties, 12ins. high, are available in most shades. The dwarf sorts, 6ins. tall, can be used for edging or for bedding. A particularly attractive strain is Twinkle, which is very compact in habit and brightly coloured. Plant dwarf types 6ins. apart, the large-flowered 9ins. apart.

Salvias.—These should not be planted out until early June for, if set out earlier, frost damage can occur. Plants grown in pots are best. Plant 12ins. apart. A good variety is Fireball, which has brilliant scarlet spikes and grows 15ins. high. There is also a dwarf Fireball, 9ins. high. For a vivid splash of colour, there is little to equal these plants, which also give a long-lasting display.

Stocks.—The Ten Week varieties, very useful for bedding are available in a wide range of colours. A good type is the Giant Perfection which has a branching habit, grows 18ins. high and plants of which should be planted 12ins. apart. Pink, red and blue varieties are most popular. The Giant Rocket type, which is of non-branching habit, 2ft. high, is also useful. It is possible, if one raises plants oneself, to obtain a type (The Hansen Strain) of which the double-flowered plants can be picked out when in the seedling stage, these being lighter than the plants which will give single flowers.

Zinnia.—These very colourful and attractive plants do best in a dry summer, on light and medium types of soil. Plants should not be put out until danger of frost has passed. Zinnias give the best display in a large bed or border. The Giant Double, and the Chrysanthemum-flowered types are 2½ft.

high and should be planted at 12in. spacing. The miniature Pom Pom types, 9ins. high, are compact in habit, and should be planted 6ins. apart. Choose an open, sunny well-drained site for these plants.

A Selection of 20 Good Subjects for the Rock Garden.

The following plants are all fairly easy to grow, and can be considered for a new rock garden, or for making up gaps in an existing rockery. As rock plants are sold in pots, or ex-pots, they can be planted at any time of the year, even when in flower. The most convenient time for replanting, however, is autumn or early spring.

Aethionema, Warley Rose.—This grows 6ins. high and is a very dwarf shrubby plant, which bears pink flowers in May and June. It does best in a sunny position and must have good drainage. It makes a bold display and is one of the most popular plants for the rock garden.

Alyssum saxatile.—This golden yellow plant, a favourite spring-flowering subject, often shares pride of place with Aubretia. Propagation is done in the same way, and a few plants of this outstanding subject should be planned for on every rockery. It is 9ins. high and flowers in May and June, giving a mass of colour in striking fashion.

Anemone.—Some of the species are very valuable in a rockery and A. Appenina, an appealing blue, 6ins. high, flowering in March and April, is very suitable. It is also useful as a plant for shady places. Bulbs should be planted in September, 3ins. deep and in a group of three or four for maximum effect.

Armeria.—The well-known "Thrift", which grows so happily on cliffs and near the sea, is one of the Armerias, but for a rock garden choose the variety Vindictive. This has rose crimson flowers and grows about 6ins. high. It needs full sun and a dry position to flower at its best, in May and June. It is an ideal rock garden plant, one that should always be included if choice is restricted.

C F G—9

Aster Alpinus.—This is a very striking dwarf aster, being 9ins. high and bearing violet blue flowers in May and June. This plant does well under most conditions, being easy to grow and very free flowering.

Aubretia.—These subjects can be raised from seed or bought as plants in pots. Seed should be sown in May or June and the seedlings pricked out into 3in. pots. They are grown on for the autumn and winter, and can be set out when in bud or when just coming into flower, in early spring. After flowering, cut off all the spent flower heads and trim back any straggly growths, especially on plants that have been in position for some time. If some named varieties are being purchased, Crimson Queen; Carmine Crimson; Dr. Mules, deep violet blue; Royal Lavender, and Dawn, rose pink, are amongst the best. Cuttings can be taken from selected plants, using the new shoots, in summer, and rooting them in a cold frame in a sandy compost.

Bellis Dresden China.—This miniature daisy with a shell pink, double flower, is of very neat habit. It is 3ins. high, flowers from April to June and always attracts attention.

Campanula.—There are many species and varieties and to select just one is difficult. If the choice is the variety G. F. Wilson, which has violet blue flowers in July and August, pleasure is assured. This plant is 6ins. high and very free-flowering.

Cotyledon Simplicifolia.—A useful subject for July and August flowering, with striking sprays of golden yellow and a neat rosette of foliage. It is 4ins. high and does well in most situations.

Dianthus.—These rock pinks need a well-drained position in full sun, and ample lime or old mortar rubble in the soil. A useful hybrid variety is The Dubarry, which has double rose flowers with crimson centres, and is of very neat habit. It is 4ins. high and flowers in June and July. Mars is a very free-flowering dianthus, 6ins. high, which bears double

130

crimson flowers from May to August. If a special pocket is made up for dianthus, use one part each of soil, old mortar rubble and coarse grit. Cuttings can be taken in summer and, indeed, it is a good plan to propagate from these plants regularly, so that young plants are always available.

Erinus Alpinus.—This is a very good plant for a dry position and its rose pink flowers are very attractive. It is 3ins. high and flowers in May and June.

Gentians.—One of the most popular group of rock garden plants but one that does not always give good results. A good variety is G. Acaulis, which has vivid, blue, trumpet-like flowers in May and June. This plant needs rich, firm soil and a special pocket made of one third compost, one third good soil and one third coarse grit will give it the conditions it needs to thrive. Another good variety, this time for August and September flowering, is G. Septemfida Gigantea. This has large blue flowers, several on a spike, and is 9ins. high. It should have the same soil conditions as G. Acaulis, and can be relied upon to give a bold splash of colour in early autumn.

Gypsophila Repens, Letchworth Rose.—This is a small trailing plant, with neat rosy pink flowers which are 4 to 6ins. high. It looks well over-hanging some stone or rock and gives a pleasing splash of colour in May, June and July.

Lithospermum.—The variety Grace Ward is well known and very popular. It has gentian blue flowers and does best in lime-free soil. It is a small, trailing plant which should have a place on every rockery. A special pocket of peat, leaf mould and grit, in equal parts, should be prepared for this valuable subject. It flowers in May and June.

Narcissi. (Miniature).—Many of these are suitable for planting in a rockery and fuller details are given in Chapter 5. Some especially attractive species are N. Bulbocodium Citrinus; N. Juncifolius; N. Triandus Albus (Angels Tears) and some of the Cyclamineus Hybrids including March Sunshine,

Little Witch, and Beryl. A Triandus hybrid, Shot Silk is a "must" for the rock garden but, in any case, try and find space for at least a few of these early-flowering subjects.

Phlox Subulata.—A very colourful variety is Betty, which has salmon pink flowers, borne in profusion during May and June. It is 6ins. high and does well in most conditions. There is a wide range of varieties available, which collectively make a valuable contribution to the rock garden in early summer.

Primula Juliae.—For early flowers in March and April, this dwarf subject with its crimson blooms is most useful. It grows 3ins. high and the flowers are borne in profusion. It thrives best of all in a pocket of half compost and half coarse sand.

Roses (Miniature).—Room should be found for one of the miniature varieties, of which the most suitable is R. Rouletti. This has small, pink flowers in June which, as they fade, should be cut off with small scissors. Choose a well-drained position for this little gem. The only pruning needed is to shorten the main shoots to keep the bush neat and compact.

Saponaria Rubra Compacta.—This has a long flowering season, from May to August, and bears bright carmine flowers, giving a colourful display. It is of dwarf habit, being 2ins. high.

Saxifraga (Kabschia Section).—These are neat cushion-habit plants, which bear brightly coloured flowers in spring. The variety Riverslea is crimson and of dwarf habit, neat in growth and makes a bold display. It needs a pocket of gritty soil and very sharp drainage for best results. A very early-flowering variety is Mother of Pearl. This has pink flowers, in February and March, and is a good plant to bear in mind for extending the flowering season of rock garden plants.

Chapter IX

Pests and Diseases of Flower Crops.

1. Principles of Pest Control, Biological Methods, Hand-picking.

2. Some Pests of Flower Crops, Sucking Insects, Caterpillars. Soil Pests. Other Pests.

3. Fungus Diseases, Soil Diseases and Virus Troubles.

Principles of Pest Control.

In general, it must be remembered that well-grown and well-tended plants, raised in soil which has had adequate dressings of compost, are much less liable to attacks from pests and diseases, than those plants which have been badly grown, starved or stunted, or have received a check in growth, especially in the early stages. Whilst it is not true to say that compost-grown plants are immune to pests and diseases, many organic gardeners have found that they get very much less trouble from these sources than where plants are grown with the use of chemical fertilisers only. Bear in mind that there are several features that can contribute to unhealthy plants, e.g. poor cultivation, bad drainage, lack of rotation or overcrowding. It is a combination of several inter-related factors, which include the maximum use of compost, that contribute to sturdy, well-grown, resistant plants.

It is well-known that plants grown in a fertile soil, with a high humus content, are far less likely to be affected by deficiencies which predispose weaker plants to attack by both pests and diseases. Remember that there are many pests which spend the winter, if allowed to, in hedge bottoms, piles of old pea sticks, heaps of rubbish and plant debris. The moral here is an obvious one: compost all suitable material, burn any rubbish that can't be dealt with by composting and remove other items that can provide cover for these pests. Eliminate, for example, heaps of stones or other material which, in any case can be put to good use in the bottom of a new path. Keep hedge bases and banks clear of weeds and grass, and do not allow weeds or rubbish to accumulate in any part of the garden. A most important aspect of organic gardening is the value of beneficial effects of certain insects. Ladybird larvae, and also the larvae of the Brown Lacewing, for example, they eat large numbers of aphides and this should always be kept in mind. Beneficial insects are encouraged by avoiding the use of poisonous sprays which, as has been stressed before, can kill all insect life, both harmful and beneficial. If this safe principle is followed, one does not have to worry about being able to recognise the many other beneficial insects that occur in Nature.

There is probably, almost certainly, still much to be learned regarding the control of aphides and other pests, from plants themselves. There are indications that certain plants act as either deterrents or controls against some pests, e.g. nasturtiums against Woolly Aphis on Apples, and certain species of marigold against some types of eel-worm. It is very probable that much new information will come forward in the future, on this aspect of pest control and prevention.

Another important practical point is to watch for the first signs of attack and to take control measures, where necessary, as soon as possible. Never allow pests, such as aphides, to build up into large numbers before taking some steps to eliminate them. All that is needed is a daily (or as often as can be managed) look at the plants, with the pest or disease factor in mind.

Many pests can be controlled by hand-picking and, on a garden scale, full use should be made of this method, particularly against the larger pests such as caterpillars on flower crops, or cutworms at the roots of plants. Leaves can also be protected from leaf miner if handpicking of this pest is done at an early stage. When direct control measures have to be taken, it is important to use the non-poisonous preparations, and to avoid at all costs using dangerous poisons if one is going to work hand in hand with Nature. Some sprays kill all insects, whether harmful or not, and the great benefit derived from the many beneficial insects is then lost.

Some Pests of Flower Crops.

It would take a separate book to deal in detail with the many pests than can attack flowers; it is only possible here to deal with the more common. For convenience, these are listed under "Sucking Insects", such as Aphides which feed on the sap in shoots or foliage; "Caterpillars," which feed on the leaves or shoots; "Soil Pests," such as wireworms, which damage the roots mainly, and "Other Pests", such as earwigs and woodlice.

Sucking Insects.—These, it will be recalled, often feed on the tips of growing shoots, i.e. the most tender parts of the plant and, if allowed to multiply, can severely check or damage the plants or even kill them. Where insecticides have to be utilised, use them as soon as possible, and employ a syringe or sprayer which will apply the solution at good pressure, directly on to the insects concerned.

Some of the materials that are used to kill sucking insects are:

Nicotine.—This is poisonous to humans and must be used with care. It is however a widely-used insecticide. It is most efficient if applied in warm weather at a temperature of over 60 degrees F. It gives a very good control of aphides. Dusts and liquid preparations are available. With the latter, it is best to use a wetter or some soft soap as a spreader, to obtain maximum efficiency.

Pyrethrum.—This is obtained from a species of chrysanthemum, and is grown in Kenya in large quantities for this purpose. It is non-poisonous to humans and can be used in combination with derris, thus providing a useful control material against caterpillars as well as many species of aphides. Pyrethrum powder costs about 6/- per lb. and, where a wettable preparation is used, 1lb. in 5 gallons of water is an effective solution. Pyrethrum dust is also available. Proprietary pyrethrum preparations should be used at makers directions.

Some of the most common sucking pests are:

Aphides.—These are probably the most commonly met with of all the flower pests, and there are many different species. An aphid is illustrated in Fig. 13. They all cause similar damage however, and all can be dealt with, if needs be, by one of the above preparations. Roses and chrysanthemums are especially liable to attack, also dahlias, but one must be prepared to find some species of aphides on a very wide range of flower plants, especially in warm weather when they breed very rapidly if allowed to go unchecked. Remember that it is the tips of the growing shoots that are most likely to be attacked first, and an examination should be made regularly with this factor in mind.

Capsid Bug.—There are several species, the green capsid being one of the most common. It attacks flower crops such as dahlias and salvias. The young stages of the pest, the "nymphs", cause spots on the foliage, which enlarge and have brown edges. Another type of capsid, can cause damage to chrysanthemums, in that it feeds on the flower buds which become distorted and often one-sided. It also attacks many annuals and perennials. The keeping down of weeds in the vicinity is important as an indirect control against these pests, for weeds serve as host plants in many cases. Pyrethrum sprays or dusts will give a good control.

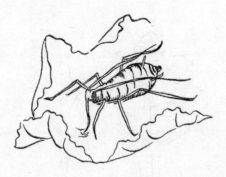

Fig. 13.—Aphid

Froghopper.—This pest which attacks a wide range of flowers is often known as cuckoo spit, due to the froth-like liquid with which it surrounds itself. Some plants frequently attacked are roses, geums and lavender which is particularly susceptible. Damage is caused by the nymphs, an immature stage of the insect which is most troublesome in May and June. It causes the leaves to wilt and can distort the shoots. It is essential to spray at a good pressure, to penetrate the "froth" with an insecticide, and pyrethrum may be used.

Greenhouse Whitefly.—There is a useful biological control measure that should be used against this pest, namely introduction of the small chalcid wasp, Encarsia Formosa. This lays its egg in the immature stage of the whitefly and the parasitic larvae feed within. The parasite can often be obtained from a tomato growing enthusiast as it is used to good effect against whitefly attacking this crop also.

137

Many gardeners are trying a few plants of African Marigolds in pots, as a deterrent against whitefly, and considerable research is being done with this use of this plant against eelworm, as mentioned elsewhere in this chapter. A plant or two of Nicandra, the shoo-fly plant, can also be grown in pots in a greenhouse as a trial deterrent against some pests that attack greenhouse plants. See also, Greenhouse Management, Chapter 7.

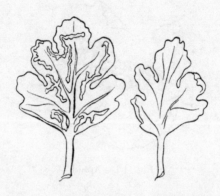

Fig. 14.—Chrysanthemum Leaf-miner.
Left: Affected leaf. Right: Normal leaf

Leaf Miner.—The larvae of this pest, (see Fig. 14), tunnel into the foliage and cause channels in the leaves. In heavy attacks the whole leaf may be damaged and plants badly checked. If the first signs of damage can be spotted at an early stage, pick off the leaves concerned. The larvae can be crushed between the thumb and finger, on a small scale. The weed, sow thistle, is also affected, so this plant should not be allowed to develop nearby, or it will serve as a source of infection.

Chrysanthemums are sometimes attacked by one of these pests, as are cinerarias. Other species can attack aquilegas, roses, sweet peas and azaleas. A useful deterrent on the foliage of plants liable to be affected out-of-doors, is old, well-weathered soot, which can be sprinkled on lightly, when the leaves are damp.

Thrips.—These "thunder flies" cause a mottling on the foliage where they suck the sap during feeding. Plants attacked include chrysanthemums, roses and many pot plants under glass, e.g. cyclamen, fuchsias and begonias. In this latter case, frequent syringing with cold water is a good control, but this must be applied at good pressure. Out of doors and under glass, spraying with pyrethrum is effective. Warm, close weather often brings on attacks very rapidly and damage should be anticipated under these conditions.

Caterpillars.—There are many different types of caterpillars which can attack flower crops; one type is illustrated in Fig. 15. In each case, if their presence can be spotted soon

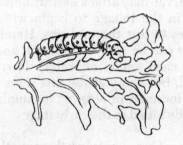

Fig. 15—Caterpillar

enough, they can be picked off by hand and disposed of. If this is not done, or if one has been away for a time, then spraying or dusting may have to be resorted to. The aim here is to paralyse the caterpillars, or to render the leaves on which they feed unattractive.

Where only a small number of plants are attacked a suitable dust can be applied from a small muslin bag, shaken on to the foliage when this is damp, as in early morning.

One of the best materials that can be used as a control against caterpillars is derris. This can be obtained as a dust, or in liquid form. In either case, it is non-poisonous to humans and animals. It is, however, toxic to fish, and should not be used near ponds or streams, where there is a danger of it

139

reaching the water. There are many other materials that can be used but some are poisonous. Derris can be relied upon for controlling caterpillar attacks on flower crops.

Some of the more common pests in this group are:

Angle-shades Moth.—The larvae (caterpillars) attack a wide range of flower crops, including gladioli, chrysanthemums, dahlias and many herbaceous plants. They are about 2ins. long, brownish-green in colour, with a pale stripe along each side of the body. They eat leaves, buds and flowers. Watch for the first signs of attack, when early infestations can be removed by hand-picking, otherwise use derris sprays applied as soon as possible.

Cabbage White Butterfly.—In addition to feeding on brassica plants, the larvae may attack nasturtiums and stocks. They eat small holes in the foliage to begin with and, later, can reduce the leaves to just the mid-ribs. Handpicking is effective or the plants can be sprayed with salt and water (2ozs. of common salt to each gallon of water). Derris or pyrethrum can also be used, but spray at the first signs of attack before the caterpillars increase in size, or in numbers, as they are much more readily killed in the early stages.

Tortrix Moths.—One species of these moths attacks young leaves and new shoots of heleniums and phlox and some other herbaceous plants. It spins the shoots together and causes considerable distortion. At the first signs of attack, pinch the larvae between thumb and finger or pick them off. It is not easy to kill them by spraying once they are within the protection of the leaves they join together.

Other species of caterpillar may be found, but in all cases, the same methods of control, as suggested above, may be employed.

Soil Pests.—

Wireworms.—These damage the roots of many subjects and cause wilting or even the death of plants attacked. They are particularly troublesome on new land, i.e. that which was recently grass turf. In such cases, aldrin dust at 1oz. to each square yard, before seeds are sown, or plants are put out, is often used. This dust should be hoed into the top few inches of soil during the initial preparations.

Where wireworms are troublesome on established plants, try trapping them by pushing pieces of carrot or potato, into the soil around the flower plants, and taking these "baits" up each day, to see if they contain wireworms. If they do, drop the whole in a tin of boiling water.

Millipedes.—These feed on the roots of many flowering plants, and may attack seedlings or mature plants. Bulbs are also liable to damage. There are differing types of millipedes but all curl up when disturbed and resemble a watch spring in appearance.

The control measures are to trap on a small scale, with pieces of potato or carrot set just beneath the soil surface (remove the "traps" when millipedes collect in them), or to apply aldrin dust to the soil between attacked plants, and hoe it in.

Napthalene can also be used against these pests (also against wireworms). When applied to empty ground the rate of application is 3ozs. to each square yard. Napthalene is still a useful material to use where damage from soil pests has to be dealt with.

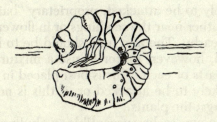

Fig. 16—Cockchafer

Cockchafers.—These large white larvae (see Fig. 16) often found in soil that was recently grassland, may attack the roots of many flower plants. Normal cultivation exposes many to birds and indeed, as the ground is brought into cultivation,

141

this pest, finding the new conditions not to its liking, is considerably reduced in numbers. Trapping with pieces of potato buried about ¼in. deep will help, if the traps are examined early in the day before the larvae go deeper into the soil.

Woodlice.—It is said that if toads are placed in a greenhouse where woodlice are a plague, they will clear this pest, but I have no first hand knowledge of this method of control. Woodlice are usually associated with wet conditions, as under stones, beneath rubbish or in shaded positions in a greenhouse. They cause some damage to roots of certain plants, particularly to ferns in a greenhouse, if these are not well tended. Some herbaceous plants can be attacked also at the roots. Trapping can be resorted to if necessary, by means of flower pots loosely filled with damp moss or with scooped-out potatoes. No decaying pieces of wood should be left lying in the garden, or any other rubbish be allowed to accumulate which could attract these pests and give them shelter.

Slugs.—These are most troublesome in damp, warm, weather, or where the conditions generally are damp, or plants are shaded. Slugs of one type live mostly below ground and are difficult to control for this reason. Those which live above ground, i.e. the ordinary type, are most active on warm, dull nights and, if trouble is anticipated and young seedlings are most likely to be attacked, proprietary "baits" can be set in position, either near the seedlings or in flower pots lying on their sides nearby. The aim here should be to keep the baits dry. I would, however, prefer to use a mixture of lime and soot, equal parts of each. This is best placed in a ring around the plants likely to be attacked or, if this is not possible, on the soil amongst the plants.

Subjects known to be susceptible, including delphiniums, can have a ring of fine ash placed around them, and even over them, in winter, but this needs replacing or rather renewing when the first applications become wet. The principle of these deterrent materials, is to give the slugs conditions over which they cannot travel freely. With this in mind, dry wood ash, is a useful material to use, but needs to be renewed after rain.

Other Pests.

Earwigs.—These, especially troublesome on dahlias and chrysanthemums, damage the flowers by eating the petals, thus giving mis-shapen blooms. They feed at night, which means that they sometimes go un-noticed, and one cannot immediately account for the damage.

A well-tried method of control is to trap earwigs by inverting flower pots on canes stood in the ground between the plants, and filling the pots with hay, soft straw or even crumbled newspaper. The earwigs gather in this protection by day, and both they and the trapping material can then be collected and immersed in boiling water.

Chafer Beetles.—The adult May bugs or cockchafers are a familiar sight in May and June, when they may be present in large numbers. They attack the foliage and buds of roses and, during the evening, can be shaken from the plants being attacked, or handpicked. If spraying is done, derris is an efficient control measure.

Eel Worm.—Mention has been made of the trial work being done at present with the growing of African Marigolds as either a control, or a deterrent, against this pest.

The most frequent cause of trouble may be with chrysanthemums. If plants are affected, the lower leaves turn black and blooms may be distorted. Commercial growers dip the stools from which cuttings are to be taken, in warm water at 115 degrees F. for 5 minutes, thus ensuring a clean start with the newly-propagated material.

If new plants are purchased, make sure that they come from a clean source. Infected plants should not be used for cuttings, unless the warm water treatment is given.

Phlox can also be affected by a species of eel worm. The taking of root cuttings can be used as a method of propagation which ensures clean stock. Plants are lifted in winter, and 3in. long pieces of root inserted in a cold frame, either flat, and covered with ½in. of a half soil, half compost mixture, or inserted upright, tips level with the surface, 3ins. apart.

Diseases.

The most common troubles are those which affect the foliage, and thus cause a severe check in growth, unsightliness or, in bad attacks, the death of the plant.

It is well known that plants which are of a very soft nature, i.e. over leafy, due to over feeding with nitrogenous fertiliser, are very much more likely to be attacked by fungus troubles than are sturdy, well-grown plants which have received an adequate supply of potash, although the presence of this latter factor will not guarantee immunity.

One of the materials used against fungus diseases of foliage is Bordeaux Mixture. There are several different variations in the make up of this fungicide, but a usual mixture is 8ozs. of copper sulphate and 8ozs. of hydrated lime to 5 gallons of water. The copper sulphate is dissolved in water, in a wooden tub, and the lime in a separate vessel. Add the copper solution to the lime, stirring well. Test with blue litmus paper, and add more lime if the litmus paper turns blue. Strain the mixture and use the same day. One can purchase the necessary ingredients in the same package, in two sections, and here, makers directions should be followed regarding mixing for use.

Other diseases which may appear are :

Botrytis.—This disease, which can affect chrysanthemum blooms under glass, and cause the petals to "damp" and rot, is very largely due to insufficient ventilation and too damp an atmosphere. The spread of the grey fungus spores can be minimised by cutting off infected blooms and avoiding shaking the spores on to nearby plants. If this trouble appears, keep the atmosphere rather drier and do not wet the foliage whilst watering.

Rust of Antirrhinums.—This disease can be serious enough to damage severely the foliage. The symptoms are dark brown spots on the undersides of the leaves. Foliage can be so badly affected that it becomes "scorched" and the plants die off.

Fortunately, where this disease is troublesome, there are now resistant varieties, e.g. Wisely Golden Fleece, which is yellow with a pink flush; Pink Freedom, and Wisely Cheerful, which is also pink. This is the best answer to the problem.

Rust of Chrysanthemums.—This may put in an appearance under glass, particularly if plants are not given sufficient ventilation. The chocolate brown spots on the undersides of the leaves cause a severe check to the foliage and the entire plant is weakened. When the plants finish flowering, make sure that no infected leaves are left in the greenhouse, under benches, pipes or staging, where they might serve as a source of re-infection the following year. Dusting the foliage with yellow sulphur is of some benefit, but aim at growing the plants sturdily, with ample ventilation, and pay close attention to watering.

Rust of Sweet Williams.—This disease is common in the southern counties, and appears as brown spots in the undersides of the leaves. The varieties with dark red flowers and dark foliage are very resistant. Set the plants so that there is a good air circulation between them and aim at sturdy growth.

Soft Rot of Iris.—This is not uncommon. The foliage of attacked plants turns yellow at the edges and, later, the rhizomes decay. This disease is worst in wet, heavy soils, especially if drainage is poor. These conditions should be corrected and new plantings, the rhizomes planted shallowly, made on a drier site.

Mildews.—There are several species that attack a fairly wide range of plants. Often mildew is induced by very dry conditions; an example of this is the mildew found on michaelmas daisies. If the plants are well grown, and obtain adequate moisture from compost dressings, little or no trouble is experienced. At the end of the season, make sure that no infected foliage is allowed to remain on the crowns of the plants, should the trouble appear in late summer.

Chrysanthemums under glass can be affected by the trouble, induced by draughts and dry conditions. A light dusting with yellow sulphur on the foliage will help.

145

Soil Diseases.

So far as flowers are concerned, the trouble most frequently met with is "damping off", which affects small seedlings grown in pots or boxes. Where this method of propagation is employed as under glass, make sure that clean water is used, especially if this is being taken from tubs or tanks.

The use of sterilised soil such as that in J. I. Composts, should ensure freedom from these diseases. On a small scale, one can partially sterilise the seed compost being used by saturating it with boiling water and then allowing it to dry out sufficiently before sowing the seeds concerned.

In severe cases, the boxes or pots can be watered with Cheshunt Compound (1oz. in 2 gallons of water), but this measure will not cure seedlings already affected. The symptoms of attack are: the rotting of the seedlings, at soil level. Large patches can be affected in a seed tray, resulting in a total loss of plants. Where losses have been experienced with small seedings, coat the surface of the seed mixture with ⅛in. of fine sand and cover the seed with the same depth. Make sure that too much water is not given and that clean cans are used.

Wilt of Asters.—There are two types of wilt disease which affect these plants. One is often called "blackleg" which causes the stems to turn black at soil level and the plants to wilt and die. A heavy soil, especially a heavy, wet soil, will cause serious losses, particularly in a wet season. All infected plants should be pulled out, and asters should not be planted on infected soil for at least 3 or 4 years.

Wilt, caused by a different fungus, gives similar symptoms, but there are now several wilt-resistant varieties available, and full use should be made of these.

Virus Troubles.

The two crops most likely to be affected, in each case by more than one virus, are chrysanthemums and dahlias. To describe the symptoms of each would take almost another book but, in general, affected plants become stunted or flowers distorted and so severely checked that they are useless.

It is essential, with both these subjects, to purchase plants from a clean source, so that no virus-infected material is introduced. Do not take cuttings from plants known or suspected to be showing virus symptoms.

Aphides and other sucking insects can spread these troubles by sap transference, as may taking out side shoots from affected plants and carrying infected sap on the fingers to neighbouring subjects.

Virus-infected plants should be removed before further infection can take place. So long as it is certain the material will be well heated up in a properly made compost heap, it can be used for this purpose; if doubt exists, I would prefer to burn such infected material.

Chapter X

Weed Control in The Flower Garden.

1. General Points.

2. Mulches as a Weed Control.

3. Weeds on Lawns.

4. Weeds on Paths.

5. Special Weed Problems.

General Points.

In general, the weed problem in some parts of the flower garden may not be so acute as elsewhere. With close growing plants (as in a bed of summer-flowering subjects), many weeds are suppressed by the density of the flower foliage, but close attention to weed control in the early stages is still essential.

Often, in vegetable growing, one can tolerate a certain amount of weed growth, as this may act as protection in winter. In the flower garden, a harder attitude has to be adopted.

Sometimes, however, it is possible to make use of weed growth. An empty flower bed can be allowed to develop a crop of weeds in late summer, then the whole be dug in, before they seed, to act as a "green manure". Chickweed forms a heavy "mat" of growth, and I have often used it effectively for this purpose.

Remember that some weeds are acid-loving plants. If any of the following are prevalent, they serve as a guide to the fact that lime is needed in the soil concerned, unless in a lawn, where slightly acid conditions are best. Some examples are: daisies, scentless mayweed, plantains, sheep sorrel, sow thistle, coltsfoot and wild pansy.

Perhaps the worst problem in the flower garden is a herbaceous border that is badly weed-ridden. Such an area is often best re-planted, even if done a little at a time. This does give the opportunity of digging deeply and removing at least the bulk of the weed roots as the work proceeds. If the worst part can be left unplanted over the following summer (fallowed), so much the better, as this allows unrivalled opportunity to dig out perennial weeds and permits repeated hoeings. A fine, warm, summer is ideal for maximum "fallow" effects.

Mulches as a weed control.

This is a very good method of weed suppression. Before it is used, pull out by hand as much weed growth as possible, in spring, whilst the herbaceous plants are small, then put down a thick mulch of lawn mowings as a weed "smother". Sawdust can also be utilised, but to guard against nitrogen shortage, as the sawdust rots down, mulch first with a generous layer of compost (if not already done).

Spent hops can also be used, or a mixture of equal parts lawn mowings, sawdust and spent hops. Some of the stronger-growing perennial weeds may grow through even a deep mulch, but considerable suppression will be obtained by this method. If the area is small, try and dig out as much weed root as possible before the mulch is applied.

If the area is large, hoeing rather than hand pulling may have to be done. In such a case, hoe off as deeply below soil level as possible to weaken weed growth, and repeat this as many times as practicable.

The same principle can be adopted with annual borders, bedding plants, roses, dahlias and chrysanthemums, i.e., keep a permanent layer of mulch material over the surface compost in summer. Even a thin layer helps; even if mulching material is in short supply, make as much use as is practicable of this method of weed control.

Weeds on Lawns.

Weed control here has nowadays become almost completely given over to the use of chemical (selective) weedkiller materials. These have the advantage of killing broad-leafed weeds but leave the grass unimpaired. Such material may be referred to as containing M.C.P.A. or 2.4.D., but in either case, if used, follow the instructions to the letter. If possible, keep an old watering can solely for use with selective hormone weed killers. There is then no risk of damage arising to crops if residues are left in the can or rose.

Lawn sand was widely used, especially before the arrival of hormone-type weed-killers. This, a mixture of sulphate of iron sulphate of ammonia and sand, is applied during the period from March to September. It readily kills the broad-leafed weeds such as daisies and plaintains, but blackens the grass for a time. If made up at home, a suitable mixture is as follows 3lbs. sulphate of ammonia, 1lb. sulphate of iron, and 20lbs. lime free sand, used at the rate of 4ozs. to each square yard.

Much can be done for weed control in lawns by cutting off the plants with a flat growing habit, such as plantains, with a knife. In a small lawn area, daisies and dandelions can be dealt with in the same way. Try to cut out some of the roots as well, for, if the top growths only are cut off, further foliage can arise from the remaining roots.

Weeds on Paths.

The harder the surface of a path, the less weeds there will be. Keeping the surface firm, by rolling, is a good practical method of indirect weed control. In the same way, if one avoids treading soil on to a path, there will be less trouble from weeds. The same applies to using barrows, or tools, and leaving a soil deposit in which weeds can grow. Sweep up loose soil or compost regularly, to prevent this.

If the path surface is of loose material, and cannot be kept firm, then frequent raking to disturb any weed seedlings is a good control measure.

If dealing with a neglected garden, the paths of which are covered in weeds, skim off the upper crust of the path surface and renew this with fresh ash, clinker or gravel. If much perennial weed growth remains, then use of a chemical weed-killer may have to be resorted to. Do not apply this too close to the soil verges on either side, as there may be danger, with some materials, of "creeping", and plants growing alongside may be damaged, or even killed.

Some Special Weed Problems.

It is important with weeds that flower and "seed" quickly, such as groundsel, to pull them up and get them to the compost heap before the seeds are formed, or the population may be increased very quickly. (One year's seeding is said to make seven years' weeding.)

Bindweed needs an especial mention, for it is one of the most persistent weeds. In a border, it can only be pulled out when seen, the plot be mulched with sawdust or lawn mowings and, in winter cultivation, as much root as possible be removed by hand.

If one has a patch of nettles to deal with, aim at cutting off the new growth in spring, when it is but 6ins. high. Repeat

152

this treatment several times, but make full use of the nettle foliage in the compost heap, as it is particularly valuable in this respect.

Many perennial weeds, including convolvulus, thistle and ground elder, are deep rooted. Pulling up as much top growth as possible will serve to weaken subsequent growth, but not kill the plant, and a programme of patience and regular hand pulling may have to be adopted. The important point is to pull up as much of the early growth, as possible. Very deep-rooted subjects, such as docks, should have as much of the root dug out, as is feasible, for merely cutting the tops off, is not sufficient. Patience and persistence will do much to keep down weeds.

Index

INDEX

157